FORBIDDEN LOVE &
GUILTY PLEASURES

BY ALI MURRAY

***

To all victims of abuse, survivors of abuse, friends and family and colleagues who have helped survivors of abuse – I thank you and ask you to continue your good work.

For every abusive person, there are ten good men and women waiting to help you if you are brave enough to reach out and ask for help. Amongst these ten people there is at least one good man or woman who will step in to help you even if you haven't asked for it – if they just knew what was going on.

***

This is a work of fiction, with real insights into the dysfunctional, sad, explicit and funny things that can happen on the journey of life, especially on the road to recovery from abuse. Names, characters, places and incidents are fictitious. Any resemblance to actual events, locales or persons, living or dead, is entirely coincidental.

No part of this publication may be reproduced or transmitted in any way without the express permission of the AMRC Concultancy (Pty) Ltd www.amrconsultancy.co.za.

All materials in this book are copyrighted.

***

Foreword by Author Ali Murray

Forewarned is forearmed

I have written Forbidden Love & Guilty Pleasures because it is my sincere wish for people to have a sense of how deeply and how severely abuse and related issues impact on people's lives. Explicit sections of this book may resonate, titillate, jar, or shock you, as I am speaking about what really happens, not what is "socially acceptable".

There is nothing nice about abuse, and by the same token, survivors may take on behaviour that is unconventional. A body and mind that has not received the correct therapy after a traumatic event will instinctively try to "self-medicate" in an attempt to process and recover from what has happened.

You are not a bad person if you have done a few wild, off-the-wall, dysfunctional, "unsaintly" things, maybe even a few hell- and hair-raising things on your journey to recovery. Underneath all that self-destruction is a good person who has had a bad experience. You can recover, restore your dignity and grace and take your power back with the right support and guidance.

I have been privileged to work with many people who were brave enough to share their life stories with me, including what had caused them to get to their breaking point and the turning points in their lives. From a counselling point of view this has enabled me to help them to find the constructive, pro-active and positive solutions they were looking for, to overcome their traumatic pasts, to recover and to win.

Whether we have been abused or not, we have all experienced heartbreaks, disappointments and levels of relationship problems in our lives. It's not the issue, but how you sort it out that's important. Just think! If you were able to let go of fear in your life, how much more would you be able to achieve?

Help is at hand, have the courage to reach out and ask for help.

Warm regards

Ali Murray

About The Author

Ali Murray is a counsellor, relationship consultant, mentor and professional speaker dedicated to assisting people with their inter-personal relationships. Ali matriculated from Roedean School (South Africa) in Johannesburg and was a Rotary exchange student in Argentina before graduating in public relations and qualifying as a paramedic in 1998.

In 2000 Ali moved into the counselling field, concentrating on relationships and intimacy. She studied through the University of Sydney (Australia), while simultaneously training as a public speaker. She has now been mentoring and counselling individuals and couples – and speaking professionally – for more than 15 years.

Ali works closely with medical and legal professionals, including psychiatrists, psychologists, social workers and attorneys, helping people to achieve and maintain successful relationships. She's also a media favourite and enjoys regular coverage on TV and radio, and in glossy magazines and newspapers.

info@alimurray.co.za
www.alimurray.co.za, www.alimurray.com

***

Author:	Ali Murray | www.alimurray.co.za
Editor:	Hagen Engler | www. hagenshouse.com
Proof reader:	Audrey Wilson
Design:	Dylan Seegers | www.atomiceighty.co.za
Legal terms contributor:	Schindler's Attorney's | www. schindlers.co.za
Photography:	Andrew Howes Photography | www.ahphotography.co.za

***

I T WAS A warm, lazy Saturday. The late-afternoon winter's sun caressed the back of the couch on which 35-year-old Jinny stretched her long limbs. She was six feet of gregarious, brunette attitude. In her teens she had exhausted a string of boyfriends with her bubbly spirit and relentless energy. She was the kind of girl both men and women gravitated towards. And yet for all her admirers, there was something lonely and aloof about her.

Luke had inherited her brown hair and blue eyes. The chubby eight-year-old lay next to Jinny on the couch watching TV. Skyla, the feisty three-year-old, was having her afternoon nap in her bedroom. They had the house to themselves, with Justin out on a trail run.

Jinny's thoughts wandered to her husband, the way Justin's hands felt as they caressed her body, the way she felt when he was on top of and inside her... He was a handsome man, intelligent, athletic, toned, well hung, and well spoken.

Now 45, his character had grown so much richer over the years of their marriage. There was so much about her Justin that she loved, and yet there were some things about him that she had begun to fear. His moodiness, his constant demands, the angry outbursts... Nothing she did ever seemed good enough. He was cordial in public but he could be so cruel in private. Controlling, critical, and cold, lacking even the most basic empathy. He was an engineer; they liked things meticulous and precise. She just needed to try harder.

Jinny would go out of her way to please him, to do things the way he wanted. In her mid-thirties, she still had her looks. They had never deserted her – even when she'd had Luke and Skyla, she had kept her figure. But she could always be thinner. Justin wished she was sexier, she could tell. If only she could look more intelligent... But lately Jinny seemed to spend more time appeasing rather than pleasing him.

Maybe Justin was having a bad year. But if she was absolutely honest with herself, they'd already had three bad years. But that's marriage. Ten years down the line, and she had more than just her own happiness to think about. The kids' well-being and security had to come first!

And all couples have their problems. Surely things would sort themselves out?

She could take the cruel, snide and unkind comments in front of others that would make her feel small and insignificant. But there was something inside of her starting to boil, something that did not want to appease him any longer. Something inside of her that wanted to break free and to scream from the rooftops, I may not be worth anything to you – but I must be worth something!

***

JINNY FELT THE cold cement floor beneath her. She felt shaky. She could hear Luke shouting.

"What have you done to my mother? You've killed my mother!"

She could feel someone shaking her. As Jinny came to, she saw her son's little face nose-to-nose with hers, tears rolling down his face. She could hear his high-pitched wailing.

"Mommy! Mommy! What have you done to my mother? You've killed my mother!"

Jinny needed to get up, she needed to protect her son, grab her daughter and run! But she felt sluggish, like she was wading through mud. She tried to get up, had to roll over onto all fours, like a dog, and then force herself up into a standing position. She was dizzy; everything was happening in slow motion. She could see Justin sitting on a chair, watching her son and waiting, waiting to slam her into the windowsill again.

Jinny forced herself to move, to move past her husband, to go inside to get Skyla. She wanted to run away, but her fear for her daughter gave her the strength to go back inside.

She screamed to Luke to run and hide, his chubby, little tear-streaked face was pale and frozen with fear. Jinny scooped up the sleeping Skyla and held her tight in her arms and ran. But Justin was at her again, pushing and shaking her, trying to get her to drop Skyla.

"You can leave if you want," he screamed. "But you'll never get Skyla! I'll lie to the courts, if I need to. I'll tell them you're a prostitute. You're not gonna leave. Who do you think you are? You just even try. I'll make you suffer for a very long time."

Jinny clung to Skyla. She would be leaving. She would be leaving now! Perhaps he would kill her. But today she would use every atom of strength that she could summon to get away from him. He was not going to get the chance to hurt and frighten the children. She managed to tear herself free from Justin's hold and ran out of the front door, clutching Skyla and screaming to Luke to run. They emerged from the house like the escapees they were. Justin's blows still rained down on her as they ran from the house.

Jinny didn't know where to go or what to do, but she needed to get away. She needed space to think. All she had was her mobile and her children. She ran to the nearest park – to the sanctuary of public view, where he would never dare to beat them. Still, they hid in the bushes, cowering, clinging to each other. He would be coming for them. Through the fog of her groggy mind, Jinny tried to gather her thoughts. She needed time for her head to clear, so she could think. What now?

Jinny needed the children to be quiet. It seemed so hard to think, and her head and face, and her arm were burning.

Jinny felt like she wanted to burst out laughing and sobbing at the same. Hysterical! Everything felt so bizarre. Out of place, out of context, unreal!

How could this be happening to her? How could her husband have assaulted her! Other husbands did this, husbands on TV, husbands in poor, downtrodden areas. Not her educated, well-bred husband! Her Justin.

Skyla was asking questions again.

"Mommy, how long are we going to sit in the bushes?"

"Mommy it's getting dark."

"Mommy it's getting cold."

"Mommy when are we going to go home?"

The trouble was, Jinny didn't know, she didn't know what to do and she didn't know where to go or who to call. After all, she was a successful therapist. Who was she going to call? People called her when they were in trouble, not the other way around!

She had to try and focus on what to do. Luke took her by the hand.

"Mommy, can't you phone someone? Maybe someone can come to fetch us. It's getting cold and dark and your cheek and your face is going a funny colour."

There are some things in life that you never forget. The birth of your children, the death of a loved one. Your husband's hands, that were meant to love and protect you, smashing into your face and body until you come crashing down.

Jinny had nowhere to go. She was afraid to call anyone. Protecting her children and keeping them with her seemed more important than telling people she had just been assaulted. Slowly she came to accept that she would have to go home. She couldn't think straight anyway, and everything was starting to go hazy again. The kids were cold and hungry and maybe Justin had calmed down. Or hopefully gone out.

She stood up. Her body felt cold, sore and stiff, like she had been hit by a car. She tried to be calm as they walked down the street. She told the kids maybe Daddy had gone out. They needed to go home and have some supper. Then they could all go to bed. But they needed to be quiet and good, or else Daddy might get into a bad mood again.

Jinny stood outside the house for several minutes looking for signs of life. Everything seemed peaceful. Maybe Justin was asleep already. Maybe he had calmed down. Maybe he would say he was sorry, that he had not meant to hurt her, that it had all been an accident. That he had lost his temper and that it would not happen again.

Jinny quietly opened the front door, Luke was trembling, clutching her hand, pleading with her, whining, please don't go back inside. But Jinny had to go back. She had nowhere else to go. The house was quiet; Justin was out. She walked to the kitchen, quickly prepared the kids something to eat and then tucked them into bed.

The bedroom door was locked. She could not get in to get her things – her ID book, her passport, her clothes. A cold chill ran through her body; she knew that he was going to be true to his word. He was going to make things long and hard and difficult for her. For tonight, she would have to snuggle up and sleep with Skyla.

****

THE MONTHS TICKED by, then a year. Jinny got used to sleeping on a mattress in Skyla's room. Justin would not let her sleep on a bed – he made sure that she slept on the floor in her daughter's room, like a slave. Ultimately, she knew that was what she had become – a slave to his moods, his desires, his whims.

She was biding her time, letting him think she was toeing the line. But that desire to break free had only become stronger. She kept repeating to herself, the first time a man assaults you, you're a victim. The second time he does it you're a volunteer. She would not be a volunteer.

She had a plan. She needed to generate more income, to save up money for a really good divorce lawyer. The laws in South Africa were changing. She was sure it was only a matter of time before high court judges awarded care (used to be called custody) of children to mothers who were prostitutes, as long as they could prove that they were not involved in prostitution at the same premises as their children. Not that she was a prostitute, by any means. She had never even had an affair! But she was not going to be taking any chances. Justin was always true to his word. So reliable.

This also meant she had to keep absolutely quiet about the domestic violence. After all, who would come to see a respected, sought-after therapist if they knew she was being beaten at home? She was good at her work; she'd assisted thousands of people with their relationship issues. She just needed a little bit more time to get everything together.

As soon as she had enough money saved up, she would put her plan into action. The months went by. It was getting harder to save money, Justin was refusing to pay for the consumables that she and the children needed. Water, electricity, food, the gardener, the housekeeper, the kids' school fees... She couldn't bear him touching her. She couldn't make love to him. She would fuck him if she had to and if it meant keeping the peace, but make love to him? That was something she would never do again.

His sexual demands had changed since the assault. He wanted to fuck her like an animal. He wanted to control her, humiliate her, dominate her. He wanted to over-whelm and consume her. But she avoided contact with him as much as she could. He could fuck her, but he could never own her.

The abuse was psychological. He sneered that she thought she was a sex therapist, but he would tell everybody she didn't even like sex. She was just a conservative little girl from the country who wouldn't even take shots up the arse for him. Now he was trying to control her with money as well. But she would not buckle. She just had to work harder and save for a bit longer.

Jinny had to mentally divide her life into two sections: the children and her work. Her work made her happy. She loved helping people with their relationship and inti-macy issues, loved helping people put their relationships back on track. She loved working with couples that genuinely loved each other, but just completely misunder-stood one another. She wished she could do the same for her relationship, but she knew it was over. Her feelings for Justin were as cold as the cement floor she had woken up on, that night when everything changed.

He was more moody and mean and malicious now. He spent his evenings at home prowling around, looking for something to find fault with. And he spent most of his weekends away riding his mountain bike. Jinny hoped he was riding more than just his mountain bike.

If he found someone else, hopefully that would make it easier for her to leave, because his focus would shift. It would not have surprised her to find her husband involved with a man. After all, he seemed to hate and despise women.

He was a woman dominator, not a woman worshipper. He did not want to please and pleasure a woman, but rather to demean, dominate and control her. Jinny suspected that the issue with women had started with his mother's drinking problem and all the wild partying. The bringing men over when his dad was out. He'd seen his mother rub her breasts in other men's faces in her drunken state. He had talked about it a lot, his mother's wild stripping parties. It was just a pity that now that he was meant to be all grown up, nothing seemed to satisfy him.

Not only was Justin screaming at Jinny, he had taken to screaming at Moya, their housekeeper, too. Couldn't either of them think? What was wrong with the two of them? Couldn't they get anything right!

At times like these, Jinny would get that feeling again, the desire to just break free. But she had to wait. Moya was a godsend. Jinny would not be able to cope with Justin's constant onslaughts, her heavy workload, and the kids, if it wasn't for Moya. Moya meant spirit, or wind in isiZulu, and Moya was like a wind. A breath of fresh air, a constant support to Jinny.

Moya had started working for Jinny when Skyla was ten months old. She was not just a caregiver and housekeeper to Jinny – they had a camaraderie. They were both 35. They each had their own difficulties to face. Moya had lost her husband to HIV, and was waging her own battle with the disease. And Jinny was just trying to keep her head above water and get through every day.

They both worked hard and did what needed to be done, but at the end of the day they could sit down to have a cup of tea, laugh and talk about life and things that still needed to be done. And how they were going to do them.

Jinny often thought she would not have been able to come this far without Moya. She often felt that Moya was her guardian, sent by God to look out for her. She was the only one witnessing what was going on, the only person she could trust with the terrible secret of what was happening at home. Moya never judged, never commented, but always supported and encouraged. And sometimes when Justin had gone out and Jinny felt stronger, she and Moya would laugh together about the cruel, unkind things he would say.

"Jinny and Moya, have you thought today? Can you think?"

And then the two of them would burst out laughing at the absurdity of the whole situation. Moya was her rock.

***

THE ONE THING in Jinny's life that gave her a feeling of complete and utter freedom was her ability to dance. As a little girl she had been mesmerised by movement, but it was the graceful, sensual dance movements that enthralled her the most. The way a body could invoke any image or experience, allowing your imagination to roam. Now you were an ancient priestess, now a village maiden. Then a swan! A mermaid! The wind! She was by no means a professional dancer, but she felt sexy and free when she moved. It was the only time she felt completely powerful and in control of her life. It was a space where her spirit could be free, where nothing and no one could break her. Dancing filled her with an inner joy that helped her to keep moving on.

Jinny had started up an amateur sensual dance/burlesque team a few years earlier. She'd got so into it that she had built a dance studio in the loft above the triple garage. The team was made up of twelve working, professional people who wanted to let their hair down. It was a chance to have a few good laughs with like-minded women and build up their sexual self-confidence and self-esteem – and maybe even use their movements to tease and please their partners at home. They laughed, cackled like kids, cried together, supported each other and built firm friendships.

There were three members of the team who Jinny was close to. Thandeka was a little younger than her, petite, feminine, graceful and gracious. She had the most beautiful soft, creamy, chocolate-brown complexion. Her hair changed all the time; she went from short weaves, to curly, to long, jet-black weaves. Thandeka was a director of a construction company and although she was petite and softly spoken, she was a strong, powerful woman who never raised her voice. She just oozed authority.

Nella was in her late twenties, with pale skin and soft features, that were in complete contrast to her long, dark-brown hair and black-rimmed glasses. She was a CA by profession, and like many CAs she spent more time in her head than she did on her appearance. There was something a little geeky about her, and yet it was her geekiness and her obliviousness to her pretty features that made her sexy.

Thandeka and Nella were the quiet girls, the girls who never really called attention to themselves. But they were consistent, steady and loyal friends. The type of girls who, if the ship was sinking, would have shouted out, "Hey Jinny, we're sinking! Pass us an oar and let's row to shore!"

And then there was Mark – almost Jinny's age, and the only guy in the team. He was their choreographer and powerhouse. When Jinny first met him, she had thought him a bit chubby, but he'd had a long-sleeved shirt on. It was only when Jinny saw him take his shirt off that she'd realised he was all muscle. And not those gym-bunny, weightlifting sort of muscles! Mark had long, strong, toned muscles, strong, well-groomed hands, green eyes and blonde hair and the funniest, bitchiest sense of humour. He made you want to roll around on the floor laughing. He laughed easily, and the girls loved to tease him. Jinny was sure they all just about drove Mark insane, because they took so long to learn the dances, and spent so much time laughing. But he was absolutely divine and they all loved being trained by him. He had such a calm, firm way about him. He was a dancer himself, an Adagio dancer actually. These dancers trained like beasts and were built like Hercules. He could hold a woman above his head with one arm and lower her down beside his body without even looking like dropping her.

When Mark held Jinny's hand as they danced, or when she was nervous before a routine and he gave her a big bear hug, she felt safe. It was like she was back on solid ground. Mark knew that she was being hurt at home – he had come early to dance one evening and had said simply, "He's hurting you, isn't he?"

Jinny had tried to deny it, but he had looked her straight in the eye and said in a gentle, yet firm way, "I know he's hurting you, I can feel it in the way your hands tremble and how your body flinches when I dance with you. I'm here for you. I won't leave you. I'll stand by you."

This was why the team adored him.

Every year the team put on a charity show to raise money for upliftment programmes for women and children. The venues and themes changed, and this year Jinny had decided on a Moulin Rouge theme. She was going to set up a massive tent in her garden for 100 guests. There would be a caterer and a bar service. A lingerie lady would be inside her home selling naughty little numbers and sexy things to the guests and their happy husbands.

Jinny knew Justin would never be physically abusive in public because he played the role of tolerant, long-suffering husband so well. So she would be safe while there were other people around. Justin had been telling Jinny for the past year that life was not about reality, it was about perceptions. And everyone perceived him as the perfect husband, so no one would believe he was assaulting her. She was also physically so much bigger than him. And if she divorced him, who would ever again come to her for relationship advice?

She knew this was going to be her last show, and she wanted to go out with a bang. These days a man had to prove that his wife was a bad mother, a drug addict or a severe alcoholic for her to lose her children. She now had enough money for a good lawyer. She was going to get away from this monster of a man.

She was a relationship consultant, not a frigging saint, and of course people would still come to see her. People came to see her because they had their own relationship problems and she had good, sound knowledge. It was sad that her relationship had not worked out the way she wanted it to. She had never wanted to be a single mom with two kids. She had wanted her relationship to work, but not all the tea in China could fix an abusive man who refused to seek help and acknowledge or accept responsibility for his own actions. She just had to get through this one last show.

***

THE GIRLS WERE training three times a week now. The dances still looked amateurish, but Mark was pushing them harder to get their moves and routines right. They would go through the dances again and again, until eventually the girls were just about doing the entire routine in their sleep. The outfits were nearly ready too! This was always the exciting part – getting your outfit; the feathers, the frills, the fuss… the preening. The sheer delight of seeing yourself transformed into a fantasy!

Part of the fantasy was making sure you had a great audience too, an audience to cheer the girls on, to party, to be generous with their donations to the charity. One of the girls had given Jinny the name of a chap to phone – Ryder. She thought he might be game to book a table for ten people. Jinny hated cold calling, she would rather stand up and talk to 300 men on erectile dysfunction than have to call someone she didn't know.

She'd tried to get one of the other dancers to call for her, but she refused. She'd had the number on her desk for two weeks and every morning she would pick up the phone to make the call and then put the phone down again. In the third week, after three cups of tea, she told herself to stop being such a ninny and make the call. She told herself if she didn't get this guy on the first call, she wouldn't call again. But he answered. He seemed lovely. Calming, soothing, and quirky. Jinny kept thinking she'd heard this voice somewhere before, so she invited him to come and see the girls dance.

A lovely gentleman in his fifties showed up at the studio, still in his work clothes. As Ryder stepped into the studio Jinny recognised him from the gym. He was the guy who came in old "Oxford" T- shirts, schoolboy shorts and pulled-up socks, the guy who never wanted to draw too much attention to himself, but who always seemed to see everything going on around him. Oh hell! One sexy dance from the girls would probably send him into a tailspin and then he'd never book a table! But Ryder stayed. He smiled, he clapped, he laughed. There was something joyous and infectious in his laugh, something that made you want to laugh along with him. And he booked a table for ten! It's was official, the show was now sold out!

With one night to go, the tent was up. The sound stage and lighting were also almost ready. The tables and chairs were set, with beautiful, bright-red ostrich feathers on the tables. The cocktail bar was in, and the girls were all atwitter with pre-show nerves. Some were compulsively running through their routines, others became snappy and bitchy… All they needed now was "Lights! Camera! Action!"

Fifty of the guests arrived in a party bus. Their party had started a few hours earlier and they were in Moulin Rouge outfits with feathers and masks, drinks in hand. The party was on!

This was just what Jinny had hoped for! Party starters, a great group to really set the tone for an evening of fun, wining and dining.

Ryder's group arrived too. She'd given him a prime table near the stage and the bar. His group seemed a bit sedate, but Jinny was sure that as the vibe kicked in, and with a bit of liquid encouragement, they would soon relax.

It was spectacular. The guests loved the pole acrobatics, the belly dancing, the singers, the duet dances, the group dances… The glitz, glamour and sparkle! Just about everybody got in on the fun, clapping and laughing and cheering the girls on. Ryder had positioned himself at the end of his table, closest to the bar and the exit, where the girls were rushing off stage to get changed for their next dance. He was right into it, cheering the girls on, smacking them on their bottoms as they rushed past, the girls squealing in delight. It all added to the excitement and fun of the evening. He'd had a lot to drink and the people at his table got louder and louder. He was laughing his infectious laugh and that got everyone laughing and cheering the girls on too. The evening was everything Jinny had hoped it would be, and so much more.

As always, she'd had a problem with Justin on the morning of the show. He had walked past her in the doorway and tried to knock her with his shoulder. But this time she had defended herself. She stuck out her elbow and jabbed him in the ribs before he got a chance to knock her off balance and into another wall. It was only one more night. She only had to put up with his abuse for one more night! But she knew his jealousy was rising again. He hated that he was not in control, that this whole show was not about him, and that the spotlight was not on him. But she hoped he would keep up his facade of the long-suffering husband for just one more night.

As the party built to its climax, Jinny rushed through to the kitchen to check up on the caterers. The guests were enjoying the buffet and going back for seconds – she wanted to make sure everything was running smoothly. She had tried to keep out of Justin's way and with all the extra people around, she was sure he would keep out of her way too. He'd far rather try to find a willing ear to listen to how hard he tried and how patient he had to be to live with a woman like Jinny.

Jinny charged through the hallway to go and change for the next dance, halting just before she crashed into Justin. He grabbed her by the arm, squeezing and gripping her until she wanted to scream out in pain. But she couldn't scream now, or even try to defend herself because a merry Ryder had wandered in, searching for the bathroom. Justin still had a vice grip on her arm. Ryder strolled over to Jinny.

"What's going on?"

Jinny tried to smile, though she was certain it looked more like a grimace.

"Nothing. It's fine," she said.

"Well, you don't look fine to me. You're coming with me."

He turned to Justin and said, "Let go of her."

Justin released his vice-like grip on her arm and Ryder summarily marched her out of the door, back to the tent.

Jinny felt such relief that she had been saved from a public scene, but she knew this would only make Justin madder. He would hurt her harder in private later. She also felt embarrassed and exposed. She didn't want anyone to know she was having a problem at home, and she hoped that Ryder had had too much to drink to remember what had happened. But she couldn't dwell on that now. She had a show to finish and money to raise – she would just have to deal with the onslaught later.

The show was a roaring success. Money was raised for the charity, and the girls had their night in the limelight. The guests enjoyed themselves and Jinny could go to bed knowing it was a job well done. The last guests left at 2am. At that stage she wished she could just sleep outside in the tent, it was sheer dread to have to go inside. She was terrified Justin would be waiting up for her, but it seemed he had gone to sleep. She crept quietly into the house and fell asleep on the couch in the TV room.

Jinny was woken by Skyla nuzzling her, like a little puppy. She was a real little snuggle bug. She had this way of creeping quietly onto your body without you even noticing, and then moulding and snuggling and nuzzling her little face into your neck while you slept. Jinny rolled over on the couch. She was cold and stiff from the dancing and rushing around the day before, still in her dancing outfit that smelt of old sweat now. But Skyla didn't mind, as long as she was next to her mommy.

"I love you, darling."

"I love you too, Mommy."

She cuddled and nuzzled Skyla some more, and they both wrapped themselves in the little blanket Skyla had brought with her. They fell back to sleep to the twitter of the early-morning birds.

Jinny heard Justin's footsteps, but she lay still and kept quiet. With any luck he would just go out. But he walked into the living room and poked Jinny on the arm. She pretended to be sleeping and tried to roll over, but he poked her on the arm again. She sat up and calmly asked what he wanted. On the inside she felt like a coil wound too tight, ready to lash out if he tried to hurt her.

He sat on a chair in front of her and looked her square in the face.

"You assaulted me yesterday morning. I want a divorce."

The assault part was laughable, but the divorce part was music to her ears. If only he knew he was set to be served with the papers tomorrow. She returned his glare, held herself back from laughing out loud.

"Sure," she said.

He was taken aback that she didn't seem absolutely devastated. He lunged forward to grab her arm, but the doorbell rang. There was silence. The bell rang again. Jinny got up with Skyla and rushed to her room to put a gown over the dance outfit.

She opened the front door. It was Ryder! He was just popping by to thank her for the lovely show. He noticed Justin standing in the passage and stepped past Jinny to introduce himself. Ryder chatted with Justin for a few minutes.

"Congratulations on the great show your wife put on."

"Mmm. Thanks."

"You must be so proud of her."

This was the second time Ryder had saved Jinny from getting hurt, but she really wanted him to go. She really didn't want Ryder involved in her problems. She barely knew him, and right now she could do without any more complications.

Jinny stood waiting for a while, then made the excuse that she had a lot of cleaning to do. She and Skyla would walk him to his car. Ryder followed them out, but as they got to his car, he turned around.

"Jinny what is going on? Are you all right?"

Jinny, was exhausted and scared and just wanted him to go away, because he was going to make things harder for her. But then she found it all pouring out of her.

"No, Ryder, things are not all right. My husband has been hurting me for a while and this was my last show. I am filing for a divorce on Monday."

"Good," he said. "Well then that's settled. We can we have lunch on Tuesday and you can tell me what this is all about."

Jeez, she thought. This man is pushy. But she said yes, because right now, right this minute, she just wanted him to go away! She could always cancel on Monday. Now he just needed to leave!

By the time she got inside, Justin had left. What a relief! Now she could tidy up, relax with the kids and file for a divorce in the morning. She felt sad and scared, and yet excited at the same time. Finally, this dreadful marriage was coming to an end. She had suspected for a while that Justin was having an affair. He spent way too much time "out riding", sending messages on his mobile, and watching programmes like Cheaters on TV. But she didn't care, because it kept him out of her hair. In a way she felt sorry for his next "victim", but she couldn't focus on that. She had to focus on getting herself and the kids out of this mess.

***

ON MONDAY MORNING, when the kids were at school and Jinny and Justin were standing in the kitchen, she calmly told him the news.

"Justin, I am filing for a divorce"

For a second he froze. Clearly his earlier threat about filing for divorce had just been a scare tactic. This was the real thing, and it shocked him. But just for a second. He lunged at her, grabbed her arm with a menacing glare.

"You can try. But I will make it agonising. You are really going to suffer for trying to leave me."

He marched out of the back door, hopped in his car and drove off to work. She did not doubt for a second that he was going to make this long and hard. But she had suffered enough at the hands of this monster. Enough was enough!

She felt a cold chill run through her body. Her palms burst into a sweat and the fine hairs on the back of her neck stood on end, she knew he was going to make her pay. She just did not know how he would make her pay. That part terrified her to the core – the not knowing, the waiting to find out.

Anyway, she had a dance class that evening, so that was something to look forward to. It was the final workout with the team for the year, and she was having it at her home studio. She was so looking forward to seeing Thandeka, Nella and Mark and to hearing all the ladies' feedback on the show. She felt drained. The emotional distress made her want to crawl into a cupboard, hide from the world and go to sleep. But she had to get through tonight. Even her closest girlfriends Nella and Thandeka had no idea that she was in any marital distress. She had managed to hide it so well. She just needed to get through tonight, and by the time they all came back from holiday, hopefully it would all be over.

That morning, while Skyla as still asleep, Jinny worked her way through to the bedroom, stuffing Justin's clothes into green plastic bags. She knew he was not going to like it; there was probably going to be a dreadful fight. She would land up sleeping on the floor like a slave again, but her lawyer had told her to get him to move out and this was the only way she knew how. She packed up all his belongings, took them through to the garage and placed them neatly in his parking space. He really was not going to like this. Jinny was afraid already. It was not going to end well, but it had to be done. She called home security and asked them to please be on the alert if she pressed her panic button.

The home security company knew about the domestic violence as Jinny had pressed the panic button on several occasions. Later she would explain it away as her being worried about a noise that she'd heard in the garden. But the security guards had seen it all before. They told Jinny that they were aware of the domestic violence problem. If she needed help, she should press the panic button and they would be there for her in a minute or two.

Justin was only due home after her dance class, so Jinny would have time to say goodbye to the team before all hell broke loose.

The last workout was so happy, and yet so melancholy. Mark and Nella stayed afterwards. Jinny wanted them to go, because she was worried that Justin would come home, but the more she tried to hurry the more they wanted to chat. Jinny heard the garage door open and her blood ran cold. She felt as if she wanted to wee in her pants. She had seen Jewish prisoner-of-war movies where people had been so scared they wet their pants. She had thought it all rather dramatic and vulgar, but as she stood in the studio listening to the garage door grind open, she felt exactly the same way. She rushed to the bathroom, where she heard the main remote gate opening. Oh sherbert, Justin was driving his car into the yard because she'd put all the green bags in his parking space. This was not going well. She rushed down the studio steps and into the driveway. She'd have to talk to Justin, to try to avert any unpleasantness while Mark and Nella were around.

But Mark saw the cold fear on Jinny's face as she ran out of the studio. He ran down the steps behind her. Jinny was standing in the driveway with Mark beside her, when Justin drove into the driveway at speed, trying to hit Jinny with the car. But Mark stepped in the way and Justin jammed on brakes, narrowly missing him. Justin got out of the car and stormed up to them.

"Mark, get out of my way. Get the hell out of here and don't come back."

Mark glared at Justin in an insolent way. Then he turned to Jinny and took his leave.

"Okay, Jinny. I'll see you during the week, then."

He kissed her on her cheek and walked out of the gate.

Justin grabbed Jinny on the arm, twisting her flesh until she felt like screaming out in pain. She didn't want to make a scene because Nella was still in the studio. She didn't want her involved in this mess. Then Nella was coming down the steps.

"Justin? Jinny? What's going on?"

Before Nella was even down the steps Justin had run up and grabbed her by the arm. He dragged Nella down the last three steps.

"Jinny, until you take my bags and go and pack my clothes back into my cupboard, I am going to hold on to Nella."

Oh my God, he was holding Nella hostage to get Jinny to do his bidding. What should she do? She didn't want Nella in the crossfire!

Nella spoke in a quiet, shaky voice. Jinny could see the tears welling up in her eyes; her neck had gone all blotchy and red;

"What's going on between you and your wife doesn't concern me. I want you to release my arm so that I can go home."

Justin gripped Nella's arm and began twisting her skin.

"Jinny," he screamed, "You better do what I say before I really hurt your friend! Nella, you're already involved. You better tell Jinny to do what I say before I hurt you some more!"

Jinny did not know what to do. She did not want to leave Nella with Justin, but she needed to get back to the studio to her panic button so she could call security.

Jinny tried to remain calm.

"Okay, Justin, just let Nella go," she said as calmly as she could. Inside she was panic stricken. "I will take your things back into the house."

He started to release his grip on Nella's arm.

"I'll help Jinny carry the bags back inside," said Nella. Still holding Nella's wrist, Justin led her into the garage. Seizing the opportunity, Jinny ran to the studio, pressed the panic button, then opened the front gate and ran into the street to wait for security. As long as Nella did Justin's bidding she would be safe for a few minutes. But Jinny could not protect Nella from Justin, let alone even protect herself. She needed help and she needed help now!

The security guard was there within minutes.

"My husband is holding onto my friend."

The guard followed her to the garage.

"Sir, please let go of the lady."

"Fuck off! I pay your salary. You get off my property."

The security guard was a tall, black man, with a patient demeanour. He decided to intervene. He stepped between Justin and Nella and wrestled her away from him.

"Sir, I must ask you to let go of the lady."

Jinny cowered behind the guard. Justin's face took on a desperate, manic look. His eyes darted about, then he turned on his heel. He stormed out of the garage and into the house. Oh my God, Jinny thought, Skyla is in the house! Mercifully, Luke was away at a sleepover. But she had to get Skyla. The man had gone mad. The monster inside him needed to be satisfied and Skyla was going to be the next weapon of choice. Jinny wasn't afraid any more, she had to protect Skyla. She ran past the security guard and into the house. She knew the shouting would have woken Skyla. She would have gone to hide under the desk in the office.

Jinny ran directly to the office. By then Justin was just behind her, she could feel his hot, angry breath on her neck. She pulled Skyla from under the desk. She had to get her out of the house. She had to get back to Nella and the security guard. Back to safety. Now completely unhinged, Justin tried to rip Skyla from her arms. Jinny was screaming now, screaming for Justin to let her go, holding onto Skyla as tightly as she could. Skyla was screaming too.

"Put her down! You're not going anywhere!"

"Leave my mommy! Daddy, leave my mommy!"

The world seemed to slow down. Three seconds felt like three hours. Jinny could see the scene before her, but it was like it was happening to someone else. It seemed surreal and unreal. But she knew she had to get away. Justin released his grip for a second and

Jinny wrenched herself free. She staggered outside to safety, clutching Skyla in her arms.

Nella had called 911 and the police arrived. Justin stormed into the garage. But when he saw the blue lights of the police vehicles, it seemed to take the wind out of his sails. He grabbed the bags, threw them into the back of his car. Revving it insanely, he screamed at her before speeding off.

"I'm gonna come back, you bitch! I'm gonna come back and I'm gonna get you."

***

OH MY GOD. This was way worse than Jinny had ever imagined. Now, not only did Nella know what was going on - she had been attacked and threatened herself. What a disaster! If Nella spoke to the other team members and people found out, Jinny could lose her relationship consultancy. That would be her whole livelihood down the drain! Then he would own her. She would be trapped by this monster forever. It didn't help that Nella was also a counselling client. Who would want to come to a relationship consultant when she and one of her clients had been attacked by her husband at her consultancy?

Nella and Skyla were both crying and shaking. Jinny had to be calm - she had to help Nella and Skyla. She could not think about herself for now. Nella had called her husband who was on his way to fetch her. Oh my God. Oh my God. That was all Jinny could think, as the shock set in. People were speaking to her, but it was as if she didn't understand the words, their voices seemed muffled. She felt tired. She wanted to go and hide in the cupboard with Skyla and wait for the rushing in her head to calm down so she could think. She had to sit down. The police and security were asking questions but she couldn't seem to understand what they were saying. She looked down and noticed she'd wet her pants. Oh my God. Oh my God. So terrible. So horrible. She had to just sit. Her legs and hands were shaking so much that it was difficult to stand.

Nella sat and talked to her, but even she was hard to understand. Something about her husband coming to fetch her. When he arrived, Nella's husband Rudi came and sat with them. He gently touched her arm.

"Jinny, my sweetheart, you're in shock. Is there anyone we can call to come and stay with you?"

Jinny shook her head.

"Jinny, Nella is going to put you into bed." He spoke to her like a child. "We're going to organise for security to stay with you guys for the night. We'll speak again in the morning."

Nella led Jinny and Skyla down to their bedroom. She helped Jinny out of her wet pants and into a tracksuit. She put Skyla and Jinny in the main bed together.

"Lock your door," Nella told her. "Security will stand guard outside. Everything else, we can handle in the morning."

Jinny wanted to cry, but she couldn't. She felt numb, apart from her arm. That was aching from where Justin had torn at it. She locked the door and waited until she heard Nella's car leave. Then she took Skyla and pulled all the shoes from the bottom of her cupboard. She crawled into the cupboard with her daughter. Then she felt safer. It was dark and the sound was muffled by the clothing. They could hide.

If they slept in the bed, Justin might come back and shoot them.

***

JINNY HAD NOT slept, but Skyla had snuggled up to her in the cupboard and made herself comfortable. She slept soundly in Jinny's arms. Such an incredibly precious child. She stirred, and her first thought was for her Siamese cat.

"Mom, we really should have fetched Snuggles, and put her in the cupboard with us." Jinny smiled.

"Ah, my sweetheart. It's is so good of you to think about keeping Snuggles safe."

"No, mom. Not to keep Snuggles safe. To keep us safe! We would have something to throw at Daddy if he found us in the cupboard. Then we would have a chance to get away."

Jinny couldn't help it. She burst out laughing and Skyla started laughing too.

God definitely has a sense of humour, if even in your darkest hour, you can find something to laugh about.

Jinny knew Nella and Rudi would be arriving soon. God what a disaster! The word would get out that Jinny had a DV (domestic violence) problem at home. They might even take legal action against her. Well, she would just have to deal with everything one step at a time.

Jinny was waiting for them when they arrived. She felt so incredibly ashamed. DV was just so low-class, so uncouth. She made them tea, then sat them down and apologised for her husband's bad behaviour. If they wanted to take legal action against her and her consultancy she would understand completely.

Nella reached across the table and took Jinny's hand.

"Jinny, you are a good, kind and wonderful woman, it is your husband who should be apologising, not you. We are not going sue you, but we are going to write an affidavit at the police station about what happened last night. We are going to stand by you. We will not be intimidated or harassed by your husband. And by the looks of things he has been intimidating and frightening you for quite some time. At the end of the day, bullies like him are just wimps who beat up on women and children because they can't beat up on anyone else."

The tears rolled down Jinny's cheeks. She did not want to cry, she wanted to be strong. But she was just completely overcome by Nella's kind strength and determination. She had been right about Nella. Nella would scream out, "Hey Jinny, pass me an oar and let me help you row to shore."

Nella had thrown her a lifeline.

"How long has this been going on" asked Nella. "Who has been helping you? Who else knows and why on earth have you kept quiet about it for so long? Do you know, the only way this is going to stop is for you to speak out about what's happening. To ask for help."

"It's my work. You know I've got the consultancy. I need to work to look after myself and the kids, so I just kept quiet about it."

"Sweetheart," said Nella, "that was your first mistake. Successful women often get beaten because their husbands feel inferior to their wives. People come to see you because you're good at what you do. They don't care if you have a problem, they just want to know that you know how to fix their problem. In fact, if you spoke out about your issues, you'd find more and more women would start opening up and telling you they'd experienced something similar. Domestic violence happens everywhere. It's like HIV, man! It's not about gender, race, religion or culture. It's about relationships going bad. The only way you're going to stop it is to ask for help."

Nella took Jinny's hand. "My sweetheart, let's at least tell Thandeka so we can both help you."

It was all just so humiliating! Jinny wasn't a stupid women, but she'd got herself into such a terrible fix. And now the truth was out. Nella knew, but instead of shunning her, she was trying to help. Still, Jinny was terrified of accepting help because she knew Justin would come after Nella and Thandeka and anyone who helped her. She didn't want to be responsible for getting Nella or Thandeka hurt. One friend being ripped around by her husband was enough for a lifetime! It had never got this bad, and Jinny felt that she still had no idea what Justin was capable of.

***

IT WAS TUESDAY, and she'd clean forgotten her lunch date with Ryder. She had planned to cancel in the morning, but with the whole green-plastic-bag drama, lunch had slipped her mind. Now it was too late to cancel, and she didn't want to be rude.

As Jinny rushed to get ready, she realised she would have to take Skyla with her. She had not sent Skyla to nursery school that morning because she knew she would tell her teacher what had happened. She'd already had to field a phone call from the principal saying Skyla had said that Daddy had smacked Mommy and that Mommy's face was blue and they had all hidden in the park until it got dark. And was Jinny all right? Jinny had very quickly learnt her lesson. Never send the kids to school the day after a beating – because kids talk!

Jinny really didn't feel like going out, but she knew that if she didn't, Ryder would be back at their house asking more questions. The best approach would be to wear her most demure clothes. She would look shabby and let Skyla run around uncontrollably. That was what she seemed to do anyway after an incident at home. Jinny decided she'd make herself as unattractive as possible and send Ryder running for the hills. Shit, it was like being a double agent! You had to keep quiet about what was going on at home and deflect any questions that might come up, all the while pretending everything was hunky dory! God she hated this, but surely it would be over soon.

Ryder was waiting for her at La Pizzeria. He was upbeat and chatty and far from being upset that she'd brought Skyla, he was actually happy about it. He loved kids! Skyla liked him too, and instead of rushing around the restaurant like a little maniac, she climbed onto Ryder's lap and snuggled. That was so out of character for Skyla – she was terrified of strangers, and here she was all cuddled up in Ryder's arms.

Ryder was so comfortable with Skyla. He moved his chair closer to the table so that he could see the menu.

"Well Jinny, what's on the menu," he asked.

"Maybe you should tell me, Ryder," Jinny replied. "Can't you read?"

"Well, actually no! I left my specs at the office. Just my luck""

"Oh, I'm so sorry."

"It's no problem. Can you tell me what kind of pizzas they have?"

She felt bad coming across a bit rude. She should be more respectful – after all, Ryder had already twice saved her from getting hurt!

Skyla fell asleep in his arms. The pizzas arrived and the two of them ate, cosy in each other's company. He kept the conversation light, asking about the consultancy. Amidst the chaos of her life, lunch with Ryder brought a semblance of order. She felt she was coming to her senses. She thanked him for the pizza, plucked her sleeping child from his arms and left.

Driving home, she began to regret not being more curious. This near stranger had saved her twice now. He was able to casually eat pizza with Skyla snuggled against his chest, and yet she knew so little about him. Was he married? What were his likes and dislikes? Did he have children?

She dreaded going home, but where else could she go? Her mobile rang. It was a blocked number, but she took the call. It was a women's voice.

"Jinny?"

"Yes, who is this?"

"You don't know me, but I know what your husband has been doing to you. I also know you are going to lose your children by Friday this week if you don't do something about it. I beg you, please go and see Marzanne. She is a female attorney, but she is the best in town."

The phone went dead. They were back again, those two words that always hit Jinny in a crisis. Oh God. Oh God. She mustn't forget that name Marzanne. Marzanne. She would do some research and phone her straight away. Make an appointment for today or tomorrow. It was Tuesday. She had two days to get this sorted out.

She arrived home, and Moya came rushing to the car.

"Madam, the sheriff of the court has just left and they made me sign this document. The sheriff says you're in trouble"

Oh God, Oh God. Jinny's hands and legs shook so badly she couldn't get out of the car. She felt like she was going to faint; her mouth had gone dry. She took the document from Moya, asking her to please take Skyla. Jinny sat in the car and opened the document. She'd never been in any trouble with the law!

It was a high-court notice of motion. There was an urgent application to have the children removed from her care on the grounds that she was an unfit mother. Proof of this was that she'd had lewd, pornographic pictures taken of herself. She had to appear in high court on Friday.

Oh God. Oh God. This man really was going to make her suffer, and he was going to make her children suffer. He was going to use the children as a weapon against her, maybe to hurt them and to make sure she was powerless to protect them. He wanted to make sure he could move back home by Friday, with Jinny safely gone. Oh God. Oh God. She had to get hold of this lawyer. Who was that women who'd called, and how did she know about Jinny? How did she know about the court application?

Jinny had only been in a courtroom once before. She remembered it vaguely. It was the day she was adopted when she was three and a half years old. The judge had seemed so very big and his desk had been even bigger. He had leaned over and asked if she wanted to go to this new family. By that stage, Jinny was already bobbing on her new dad's knee, holding her new fluffy dog toy. The kind that jumped when you wound it up and made a funny yapping noise. The light shone through the window behind the judge and he had looked like a big Father Christmas. He would have looked good perched on the top of a Christmas tree.

Today, Jinny sat at the back of the courtroom, huddled in a corner. She wanted to be as far away from Justin as possible. She wanted to hide again. She felt degraded, humiliated and petrified of losing her babies. This was why she had saved up for two years. Because Justin had long threatened that he was going to tell the judge she was a prostitute. Then she would lose the kids.

"All rise!"

The judge walked in. Marzanne Fourie and her advocate moved forward to address the judge. Mr Dimwit and his advocate, representing Justin, moved forward. Words. The judge asked if the wife was present and Marzanne and her advocate nodded and pointed to Jinny in the corner. Words were exchanged, Latin words that Jinny did not understand, between the advocates. The judge tapped his mallet.

"All rise."

Court was adjourned.

Oh my God. Oh my God. She'd lost the kids. She waited for everyone to leave and then walked out of the side door. The Urgent High Court was six storeys up. She went to stand by an open window. This high up, there were no burglar bars. She looked down; she wanted to climb out of the window and jump. She felt no fear, just that life would not be worth living if she could no longer protect her kids. It was a mother's duty to protect her children! She gripped the window… Just then, Marzanne appeared and gripped her arm.

"Mrs Pringle? Jinny?"

"What? Have I lost my kids?"

"No. You haven't lost your kids. The case has been adjourned. The judge ruled that even if you were a porn star or a prostitute, the plaintiff had yet to prove you were a bad mother. A family advocate has been assigned to the case to investigate further. The judge said that there was no urgency in this matter. He's asked the family advocate to report back to him at a future date."

How much more of this stress could she could take? She was breaking. Getting to the end of her tether. She began to sob. Deep, uncontrollable sobbing. She tried to apologise to the attorney, in between sobs. She thanked her for her help and left. She needed to get away, somewhere quiet, where no one could see her. She was just overwhelmed. Her world was not safe.

Justin could not stand the word no. This ruling would infuriate him. There would be worse in store for her. If nothing else, he was a man of his word. He had said he was going to make this process long, hard and torturous. That would come to pass.

When Jinny got home, Moya was waiting with a cup of tea, wanting to know how things had gone at court. Moya was such a godsend. She would never have been able to cope without her constant support.

Jinny thanked Moya for the tea and went to lie down. She was too tired to talk. Her head was buzzing; she couldn't think. She just wanted to lie down and hope that the world would stop spinning; hope that when she woke up, everything would be better; that this was just some crazy nightmare.

She'd been in bed for an hour when Moya came through to the bedroom with another cup of tea and placed it on her bedside table next to her.

"Madam?"

"Yes, Moya?"

"I will stay tonight until you feel better. I will be staying with you in the spare room, until you feel better."

Thick tears rolled down Jinny's cheeks again. She could not stop them and she was just too exhausted to speak. Moya put her hand on Jinny's shoulder

"Okay, Madam. Now you must rest. You have got a workshop tomorrow night. You must be pretty and happy tomorrow. I will watch the children. You must have a sleep."

There is a God. And somehow she sends her angels in your deepest, darkest moments of need. They bring you the strength to stagger on.

Jinny slept like the dead.

***

THINGS SEEMED TO quieten down for a while. Justin moved into a rented, double-storey house and Jinny hoped that the worst of the storm was over, that she could settle down with her work, get the divorce settled as soon as possible and get on with her life. It was the end of March, only one more week to go before Easter. She loved Easter - watching the kids hide their Easter eggs, then rushing around trying to remember where they'd hidden them. Finally, she'd watch them unwrap and eat their Easter bunnies — ears first. Then she'd wait for the sugar-rush chaos to hit!

The phone rang. It was a woman who introduced herself as Nora.

"Nora?"

"Yes, Nora."

"I'm sorry I don't know you. Have we met before?"

"You know exactly who I am."

"I'm sorry, I don't. Would you like to tell me who you are?"

Nora spoke with a strong working-class English accent, although she was trying hard to make herself sound well spoken.

"I'm Justin's girlfriend and mother to his son."

Jinny's heart was pounding and she felt like puking. She had always suspected and hoped that he would have an affair and get into another relationship. Ideally he'd then leave her alone. But she'd never imagined he would have another child with someone.

If this woman was telling the truth, that meant he'd been involved with her for several years already! Jinny's mouth went dry.

"I'm sorry, why you are calling me?"

"I'm calling to let you know, you vicious cow, that Justin has told me everything about you. Justin and I are going to take everything you own and love away from you! We're going to make sure you land up in the gutter!"

Jinny slammed the phone down. She was shaking. Her heart was shuddered in her chest and the room spun. She'd hoped that Justin having a girlfriend would distract him and mellow him. But being the ultimate wimp he was, he was now using third parties to do his dirty work. No doubt Nora had fallen for his poor, long-suffering-victim routine. In time, she too would probably become a victim to Justin's malicious, vicious, conniving ways.

But Nora and their son were not her problem – her problem was her kids and how to pay their way.

The doorbell rang. It was the sheriff again. She had not met him the first time he'd served papers on her as she'd been at the restaurant with Ryder. She invited him in for a cup of tea.

She'd always imagined that sheriffs would wear blue suits and badges like in the American movies, but this sheriff was dressed in a casual top and jeans. He introduced himself as Johan. She wondered if he was coming to give her a replying affidavit from the divorce summons.

Jinny prepared the tea and asked Moya to bring it through to the main lounge. She eyed the wad of papers in front of Johan. That was one heck of a lot of papers for a replying affidavit for a divorce. The sheriff had a few sips of tea, picked up the wad of papers and handed them to her. She started to read the cover page. It seemed to be from a bank.

"Is this part of a replying affidavit for a divorce or something different?"

"Ma'am, it's an eviction summons. You need to be out of your home within a week. Your home is going to be auctioned."

"I think you must have the wrong home," she smiled. "I've paid off three million rand on the bond. I only have about R20 000 left to pay. There must be some mistake! Are you sure this eviction order is for this house?"

"The eviction order is most definitely for this home," he continued, putting down his tea. "It seems all the money was taken out of the bond about 18 months ago. We've been unable to trace Justin and the payments are already 12 months in arrears."

Oh God, Oh God. The gutter. He wanted her in the gutter!

She thanked the sheriff and let him out. What was she going to do? Her dance studio and her counselling practice ran from this property! If she lost her home she wouldn't be able to generate any income. She was losing her home. Her home was being auctioned in a week's time!

How could Justin do this to her and the kids! How could he have a son with someone else! How could he involve this low-class tramp of a paramour in their divorce! Well, it was now becoming clear that once a man crosses the line and starts emotionally and physically hammering you, absolutely anything is possible.

But her immediate problem was where she and the kids could live. She would have to look for a small cottage - a big adjustment from her current situation in a seven-bedroomed, five-bathroomed house. But as long as she and the kids were together it would be okay – she would just have to start from scratch again. For now, though, she would have to focus on work. Tonight she was presenting a ladies' workshop on Good Sex in Relationships. She had a week to think about where she was going to go and what she was going to do.

***

THE EVENING WITH the ladies was going well. Jinny loved her work; she loved to see people happy and doing well in their relationships. In time she also hoped to find someone wonderful to share her life with. The girls had been teasing her all night…

"Are you going to end off your talk with a sexy stripper, Jinny?

She'd done this occasionally in the past, at the request of the bridesmaids at hen parties. But with all the hassles she was having with Justin, she wanted to fly under the radar for a bit. Just until all the unpleasantness was over.

Suddenly Jinny saw blue police lights flashing and there was a buzz on the intercom. "Good evening. South African police. We want to come upstairs to see what's going on!"

The ladies giggled expectantly as a good-looking cop with bulging muscles and a tight uniform entered. They were convinced this was their stripper. Jinny knew otherwise.

"Which one of you is Mrs Gent?"

"I am."

"Can you please step outside with me?"

One of the ladies just couldn't contain herself. She ran forward and gave the cop a big, sexy hug, running her hands down his back.

"Do you offer any extras after your dance?

"Ma'am, please let go of me!"

He was a shy one, this cop.

"Mrs Pringle, please come outside," he instructed Jinny firmly.

Jinny was afraid. Something was wrong. Was this chap really a cop or was he just posing as one? And truth be told, he did look a bit like a stripper! Had Justin sent him here to cause trouble, so that he could lurk outside and pose for some more allegedly lewd photos?

"Mrs Pringle, we have received a complaint from Childline about you. They claim that you are involved in child pornography? Is this true? Where are your children?"

"Sir, my children are in the house with their care giver. Would you like to come in and meet them, or should I be calling my lawyer?"

At this point, one of the delegates who had consumed way too much alcohol leaned out of the window and screamed down at them.

"I've been really, really bad! Why don't you come back up here and arrest me!"

More shrieks of laughter from the ladies. This wasn't helping. Oh God! If only the ladies knew that was possibly the worst thing they could have done. As she glanced down the driveway, she saw Justin's car parked outside. She could see a short, squat woman with long, greasy, home-coloured hair sitting next to him. Was that the girlfriend?

It was Justin. He had trumped up this whole thing to try to take the kids away from her again. Not because he loved the kids. He didn't! It was because he wanted to take what she loved away from her, to punish her for daring to leave him in the first place.

Within a week, Jinny was going to be homeless with no way to earn a living. Was his plan to take the kids away from her too? So that her only reason for living was gone too?

Staying on the front foot, Jinny informed the policeman that she was going through an acrimonious divorce.

"If the man who made the call to Childline was named Justin or if it was Nora his girlfriend. It was probably a malicious attempt to intimidate and humiliate me in front of my guests."

The cop radioed his superior and it seemed they suspected it was Justin who had placed the call. The cop apologised for the scene and left, to the sound of women whooping and hollering from the balcony.

"Don't go! Aren't you going to come back and arrest me?"

Oh God. What a disaster. Thank goodness the delegates were upbeat and no harm was done. In the end, everyone had a jolly good laugh and giggle about the situation. If only they knew how serious it really was!

Jinny would have to make some decisions in the morning as Easter was rapidly approaching. She and the kids were going to be homeless by Good Friday.

There was only one solution. She would have to go and live with her mom and her stepdad and their kids in Cape Town. The auction of her house was going to happen. Justin had drained the bond of all money and now the bank wanted its cash back. Justin's malicious bullying and stupidity was escalating and now he had a fired-up, greasy girlfriend to do his dirty work. And Jinny had no more money for legal fees. She had spent a good R200 000 on Justin's first urgent high court application. Everything she had saved up to divorce this monster was gone.

She had three days to tie everything up before she had to leave. She could only take as much luggage as she could fit in her little car. Then she would have to hand the keys of the house to the sheriff and let Moya go… Oh, Moya. She could just about scratch together three months' salary for her, to serve as some kind of retrenchment package.

But she was certain that she would be able to find Moya another job with a good family pretty quickly.

She remembered those movies about World War Two and how the Jews had to leave home with just the jewellery they could sew into their hems and what they could use to bargain with or carry. What was she going to take with her come Good Friday, when she started this new phase of her journey? At the end of the day, only five things were important: the kids, the cat, the car, the computer and as many clothes as she could fit into their suitcases and the car.

On Good Friday morning, the sheriff was brutally punctual. It wasn't Johan, this time. Some other guy. He was at the gate by 9am. With all the cold efficiency she could muster, Jinny handed the keys of her home to the sheriff, got into her little car with her kids and left. Ten years of marriage down the drain, a practice now on shaky ground. This was definitely not a good space to be in, but at least the kids were safe and fed. You can't always choose the life you're dished out, but you can choose to survive and win and that is what she was going to do. Survive and win – the kids needed her to survive and win!

Jinny was so tired. She just needed to get down to Stellenbosch, in the Cape, to her folks so they could help her with the kids. In a way, a good Easter weekend away from all the drama was just what she needed. The kids loved their grandparents and were looking forward to seeing them. They already seemed less anxious and relieved to get away from Johannesburg.

***

JINNY WAS GOING to need to go back to Jo'burg for work. Stellenbosch is a beautiful university town with no shortage of happy students wandering about. But what she needed was to make money. Starting up a new practice in a new town took years, and time was not on her side. She was going to have to commute. She would ask her folks if the three of them could live with them for a while, while she got back on her feet. The kids could go to the local school and once her finances were stable she'd either open a practice in Stellenbosch or move everyone back to Jo'burg again. If her folks agreed, it would be the best short-term solution.

To her massive relief, they did agree.

But she should have known there was no escape from the madness. Two weeks after Jinny, Luke and Skyla arrived in the Cape, she got a call from the Sandton police station in Johannesburg. They wanted her to come into the station as there was a warrant out for her arrest. Jinny knew she hadn't done anything criminal. But she no longer had sufficient funds for attorneys, so she would have to go back to Jo'burg and sort everything out herself. This would also give her a chance to look for office space to run her practice from. Perhaps she could start the dance team up again at a gym. But not right now; she just didn't feel like dancing any more.

Jinny flew up to Jo'burg, caught the Gautrain and then a taxi to the police station. She was certain she was not going to be at the police station for long. After all, she had done nothing wrong in driving down to the Cape with the kids. It's not illegal for a mom to relocate with her children. Obviously Justin would be livid, and no doubt he was now trying to conjure up some malicious revenge. But she had no other option for now. She needed a roof over her children's heads, food in their tummies, a calm and happy environment and a few months to figure out how she was going to get herself out of this mess.

She entered Sandton police station and reported to the officer on duty. She asked to see Detective Warrant Officer Ackerman, who had contacted her. She was directed to his office. Ackerman was a large, blonde man with a moustache. The minute Jinny arrived at his office she felt a chill in the air.

"Are you Mrs Jinny Gent?"

He used her previous married name, which she'd taken to using.

"Yes, I…"

"I'm placing you under arrest."

He turned to the policeman who was in the office with him.

"Warrant, please arrest this woman…"

She tried to stay calm. She'd done nothing wrong. She'd done nothing wrong! "Please can you tell me what am I being arrested for?'

"Theft."

"What have I stolen?"

"The contents of Mr Justin Pringle and Nora Pringle's residence."

"What?"

"Did you steal the contents of the Pringle residence?"

"No! I am Mrs Pringle! Gent is my previous married name."

"What?"

"Did Mr Pringle at any stage of his lodging a case against me advise you that I am his estranged wife?"

"No. But a docket has been opened, and it is our duty to arrest you."

"What are you going to do with me?"

"You are now going to be fingerprinted and your information will be loaded onto our system to see if you have any outstanding charges against you. Then we are going to put you in a police van and take you to the prosecutor's office. You can explain to him how this has come about. We are only officers of the law. We execute the law. We don't decide who is innocent or guilty – that's the court's decision"

So that was it. They were arresting her. She had no one to call, and even if she had, would she want anyone she knew involved in this mess? At the charge office, Jinny was fingerprinted and put in the back of a yellow police van. Like a criminal! She was taken to the Randburg Magistrate's Court, where she sat on a hard, cold, wooden bench alongside a policeman and waited for her turn to speak to the senior public prosecutor.

She knew Justin had simply found a new way to terrorise her. But now he was using the very people meant to be protecting her. If this situation was not so bizarre it would be laughable. But it wasn't funny. Here she was on her own, with no friends she could trust enough to call and ask for help, and no money for a criminal attorney. She would just have to speak to the prosecutor herself and clear this whole mess up. She refused to contemplate what would happen if she couldn't.

She waited on that cold, hard bench by the prosecutor's desk for most of the day. When she finally did see him, the fear had crept in. She was so overwrought with anxiety and fear that when she tried to talk she realised she was stuttering. She had not stuttered since primary school. Jinny started to cry. She didn't want to cry, but she couldn't help it.

The senior public prosecutor, Mr Du Preez, was a stern, intimidating presence. A tall, thin, Afrikaans man, he chain-smoked in his office. He had an ashtray brimming over with cigarette butts and his desk was flooded with blue, pending dockets.

"Why are you here, Mrs Gent?"

Jinny tried to explain what had brought her there, but again she started to cry. Du Preez dug in his desk for a tissue.

"Please stop crying. It makes me feel uncomfortable."

Jinny tried to stop. But she was so terrified that the tears just rolled down her cheeks as she tried to talk and sniff her way through her explanation. It was pathetic. But she just couldn't stop crying and shivering. She explained about her acrimonious, malicious divorce and how Justin had opened a case of theft against her without telling the police that she was actually his wife. She had no money for an attorney, which is why she was here on her own.

Du Preez leaned back in his chair, sucking on his cigarette and exhaling like a puffing dragon. The image almost had Jinny laughing out loud. But then Du Preez leaned forward, stubbed out his cigarette in his overflowing ashtray and spoke.

"Mrs Pringle, you are free to go. You have done nothing wrong. By law, even if you sold every single item of your husband's household, you could still not be charged with theft. I am going to nolle prosequi this case. In other words, we're not going to pursue it."

"Oh, my God. I'm so relieved, I…"

"But you are not to tell anyone, because on Tuesday your husband is going to appear in court with his expensive attorneys and advocates all pumped up and ready for his big kill. I am going to tell him he is not only intimidating and harassing his estranged wife, but he is abusing the police and the court system. Then I am going to ban him from ever setting foot in my courts again with this type of nonsense."

"So I can go?"

"Mrs Pringle, you are free to go. You should also consider getting a protection order for yourself and the children so you can legally put a stop to the domestic violence that you are experiencing.

Again Jinny started to sob. Du Preez handed her another tissue.

"Please. The crying. It really makes me feel uncomfortable."

"I know, I know! I just can't help it! Thank you, Mr Du Preez!"

"I'm just doing my job, ma'am."

Du Preez called the two policemen into his office and instructed them to release Mrs Pringle as she was free to go.

Jinny had arrived in the back of a police van, so she called a taxi to take her back to her friend's house. She really just wanted to get back to Stellenbosch to be with the kids, but her 36th birthday was tonight and she knew her friends had planned a "surprise" birthday party for her. She would have to stay in Jo'burg for another day at least.

How much worse were things going to get before he actually just let her go? Or was he going to continue with his onslaught forever? Until Mr Du Preez had come through for her, it had felt like no one could protect her. Now she had no idea what to expect next. But a feeling of dread and anxiety had crept in, and was starting to settle into her soul.

***

WELL. THE PARTY turned out to be a real surprise, even though Jinny had secretly known about it ahead of time. The really big surprise turned up in the form of a well-dressed, well-spoken, 6' 2" Canadian, whom the girls had organised as a "birthday present". After the type of day that she had had, a gorgeous Canadian with a nondescript name – Craig – was truly the cherry on top of her birthday cake. Still, Jinny was so mortified, she could hardly speak to the chap and apologised to him for her friends' insane thinking in organising her a date for her own birthday party. Craig seemed comfortable with himself. He just laughed, and leaned back in his chair.

"Not to worry. I'm enjoying this, and I enjoy meeting new people, anyway."

Her girlfriends were a divine group of ladies and they gave her an assortment of lovely books as prezzies. They were all about being single again and how to get back on the horse. "There's nothing like getting under another man to get over an ex," was what they kept saying.

The big freshly single reads were Act Like A Lady And Think Like A Man, by Steve

Hardy, Nice Girls Don't Get The Corner Office, and a tiny book on men who are recently single. It seemed to be about their antics and what they get up to, like being booted out of home to live in the garage, while their wives get to keep the mansions and the Porsches. Jinny was going to have a good read when she got back to the Cape.

Jinny felt blessed to have such an amazing group of friends who stood by her no matter what. Even with all the drama, she could still see the funny, positive side of life.

She was flying back to Cape Town in the morning armed with her "single and dating again" books, sans the Canadian, who was lovely but ultimately self-centred, with a booze-and-pill habit he thought he was hiding rather well. But Jinny was a counsellor after all, and could see it from miles away. Pity she hadn't seen the signs in her estranged husband before she'd gone and married him! But as the saying goes, hindsight is 20-20!

It was wonderful getting back to the Cape and the kids. She'd only been away for a few days, but it felt like centuries. Jinny needed to settle and get some focus on work. She hoped that now, 2 000km from Jo'burg, all of this vexatious litigation would stop and that the "out of sight, and out of mind" theory would apply. All Jinny wanted was that she and the kids could get on with their lives, and that she could start recovering from her own disastrous relationship in peace.

But money was a real problem. She really needed to stabilise her income. She had not seen clients in ages, so she would have to go back to Jo'burg. She just did not have the time or the money to start afresh in the Cape. Her parents had been a godsend and had agreed to help with the kids while she was in Jo'burg. Ultimately they wanted Jinny up and financially stable as quickly as possible. No one wanted them to exhaust their pension money while she got back on her feet.

Jinny had been back in the Cape for two weeks when she got a phone call from an insurance broker.

"Are you the thief who stole everything from the home in Sandton?"

Jinny laughed, "Is this a joke?"

She was sure insurance assessors were not in the habit of calling up thieves. But the "assessor" advised that a "Mr Justin and Mrs Nora Pringle" had submitted a claim for the entire contents of the home. (Had he married the bitch? Were they pretending to be married?) They had a case number from the police station and were alleging that she was the thief. Luckily for Jinny, she had received a letter the day before from Choc hospice in Jo'burg, thanking the same Mr Justin and Mrs Nora Pringle for their generous donation to their hospice. Jinny had called up to find out what it was about. She'd always wondered how Justin and Nora had been able to lodge a case of theft with the police if the entire contents of the home were still in the house. They would have had to move the furniture and appliances elsewhere before lodging the case with the police.

Jinny politely told him that this was a fraudulent claim and that she was in fact the estranged Mrs Pringle; that Nora may simply be posing as Mrs Pringle and that she suspected they'd donated the contents to a hospice. She offered to send the hospice's letter, with their list of the donated items, to the assessor for his perusal. As luck would have it, Choc must have had her ancient address at her parents' house. It had been years since she'd made any donation. God did have a sense of humour, and a sense of justice to boot. Justin and Nora's devious plans had crossed the line into criminal behaviour. So far most of what they were doing to destroy her had been blocked, but Jinny had no doubt that Justin and Nora were capable of hurting her further. They were not finished with her yet!

Not two minutes after putting the phone down, as she was still chuckling to herself at Justin's almost comical fraud, a courier arrived with yet another lawyer's letter. It was from Justin's attorney. They wanted a paternity test on Skyla. They seemed to believe that one of Jinny's professors might be Skyla's father!

Jinny began to laugh. It must have been a stress reaction! It was such wild, insane laughter. What a humiliating thing to do! This was the final straw! She had always been faithful in her marriage. This was just another of Justin's tactics to humiliate and degrade her. To try to get out of paying maintenance for the children, or if that failed, to cripple her financially and emotionally. She had no qualms about taking Skyla for a paternity test ¬– she knew full well that Justin was the father. Part of her wished the paternity test would come back saying something different – just so that she could be rid of him. But no, Justin was indeed Skyla's biological sire.

***

AFTER THE PATERNITY saga, yet another part of Jinny seemed to break. She didn't know what it was, but there was something inside her that just snapped. Her whole life she'd been treated badly by men and humiliated to her core. The calm she'd managed to maintain until now began to be consumed by a new fury, a rebellious internal rage.

Jinny knew that she needed to give her kids a stable, happy childhood and God himself knew she had not quite got this right in her last ten years of marriage. If that meant settling them in with her folks while she commuted to Jo'burg, that was just the way it had to be.

That didn't make it any easier to head back to Jo'burg like a migrant labourer, sending money home for the kids. Part of her felt it was her job, her duty to look after her kids. But desperate situations require desperate measures, and this was basically the only way to free herself and secure for her children a semblance of a peaceful childhood.

Jinny settled the kids into new schools and set off for Jo'burg, determined to make a go of things. Her friend Carol had offered to let her sleep on the couch in her study, and Jinny had accepted. What a fall from grace! Sleeping on a couch, when just a few months ago she'd had her own home, studio and consulting rooms. But who was in the mood for comfort when you were so far away from your kids! She pined for them. Every phone call to them would end in tears. Every day away from them was harder than the one before. She stopped speaking about them because the pain of being apart was almost unbearable. She couldn't sleep at night worrying how she was going to pull her life back together and get them all back under one roof.

She knew she would need an attorney on call as Justin's ever more depraved vengeance schemes revealed themselves. But who could afford one! In essence, the only way to sort out the entire mess was to make more money. Justice would only be served if she could afford to pay for it!

She moved her practice to an office where she was able to rent boardroom space by the hour. By day she helped her clients process their problems, and by night she stayed awake worrying about her own problems. Sometimes she felt like screaming at patients, with their mundane problems. She wanted to holler, "You stupid, stupid, stupid bitch! You're so damn lucky to have what you have! To still be able to spend time and money moaning about your partner, who actually bends over backwards to look after you! If he had any balls and any sense, he would dump you and go find a woman who really loved him. And you! You're just hanging onto him because you can't let go of that golden ball and chain and his wallet!"

Then there were the male clients who were beating their wives. She felt like climbing over the table and beating the snivelling wimps herself. She couldn't stand the bullies. She would refer them over to a psychologist whom she disliked intensely, but who thrived on abusive patients.

She should be seeing a psychologist herself to deal with her own issues, but she felt she was still able to deal with the patients who annoyed her without prejudicing their well-being. She did not want colleagues to know what was going on in her personal life. Colleagues talk, and she was only six degrees of separation away from someone who'd tell Justin that she was back working in Jo'burg and sleeping on a friend's couch. She didn't want people to know how badly she was doing. Maybe it was her ego, or maybe it was her desire to succeed that made her feel this way. But she didn't have time to analyse herself right now – she needed to generate income!

***

RYDER HAD INVITED her for lunch a few times and she enjoyed his company. She felt safe around him, that she didn't have to hide from him because he knew her worst stuff. He was twenty years older than her and yet there was something boyish, as well as fatherly about him. He was Welsh by descent, but had spent his teenage years in Australia and he spoke English with a pleasant Australian lilt. He would pay for lunch every time without fail, and never asked much about the kids. This would make her cry, and he clearly felt his role was to make her laugh. She found out that he was married, and that his wife had been devastatingly and horribly maimed in a car accident years before. His kids were about ten years younger than her. She felt bad lunching with a married man. But as he reminded her, she was still married too! So what difference would it make if two friends who were having a difficult time at home had a brief respite from the misery of marriage?

In a way, the fact that Ryder was married made her feel safe. He could never become possessive and overwhelming like her ex, because he had a wife - someone to go home to every day, even if she was disabled. He seemed duty bound to care for his wife. He clearly had no intention of ever leaving her, so for now he was the perfect guy friend to have around.

Jinny had brought her birthday books back with her and spent nights reading. She couldn't sleep anyway. As the gaping hole in her heart began to heal, and she could contemplate life after Justin, her books offered solace – and some practical advice. Act Like A Lady, Think Like A Man had a few great dating tips. Author Steve Harvey recommended putting men on a 90-day waiting period if you wanted to keep them long term. Within the first 90 days the marketing phase normally wore off and you could work out if the person was just there for the shag or because he genuinely liked you. If you factored in the time it took to meet someone, then by Jinny's calculations that meant you could only date three guys a year! She was nearly 37 already! So if she was going to take Steve's advice, and she didn't actually sleep with the guys, why not date three simultaneously to speed up the whole process! After all, the first book she had read – on men being single at 40 – had stories of them all dating three girls at once. Needless to say, the outcomes were sometimes a bit hairy! But there was no way Jinny was ready for a sexual relationship, so multiple dating made a lot of sense.

***

RYDER HAD INVITED Jinny to go on a typical English picnic. It sounded quite attractive – a three-course meal at a beautiful place under the trees by a river. She was looking forward to being spoilt a bit. It was so long since she had done something that was just sweet and happy.

It was indeed amazing! Ryder had organised lunch at a private game reserve just out of town. He had laid on a table groaning with French bread, roast chicken, cheeses, wine, and cheesecake for dessert. It was actually all quite romantic – apart from Ryder dashing off into the bushes every 30 minutes. It seemed the sound of the rushing river water was stimulating his urge to pee, and the wine was clearly working through his system – either that, or he was really nervous. But she forced herself to avoid counselling mode. She focused on the embarrassment factor of watching Ryder charging off into the bushes. It kind of ruined the ambience to watch him mark his territory every half an hour or so!

But still, it was lovely. After lunch, they settled down on a huge couch under a tarpaulin in the crook of the river bend. It was cool and shaded and Jinny felt relaxed and happy. Before she knew what she was doing, she leaned over and kissed Ryder on the lips. She shouldn't be kissing him, but Ryder had made her feel happier than she had been in ages! He kissed her back, and slid his hands under her top. He demanded that she take her top off. She acquiesced, but there was no ways she was going to be taking anything else off - in a nature reserve!

He kissed her again, forcefully, like he was hungry for touch and angry at the same time. He took her hand and moved it onto his groin, moaning and raising his pelvis to meet her. She caressed the front of his pants, now bulging with his hard dick. He was huge! There was something about it that excited and terrified her at the same time. She applied more pressure, using harder, more even strokes up and down the front of his jeans. He was lifting his pelvis towards her and pulling her hard, closer to him. He grabbed her hand.

"Touch me" he ordered, like he was used to women doing what they were told! She felt that rage at being controlled and dominated boil up in her again; the moment of wild, irresponsible lust was broken. She pushed herself away and stood up. She grabbed her top, fumbling to put it on, and trying to smooth it down as she did so.

"Is that it?" he asked, still panting.

"I think that's more than enough excitement for one day. But thank you for a beautiful picnic. I've got a meeting to get to."

She gave him a perfunctory peck on the cheek as he stood up, then turned and marched off. She was filled with rage, rage at herself for being so stupid. She should have known that men can't be monogamous, even when they're twenty years older than you. And rage at Ryder for being married but unable to be faithful. All men are the same, no matter how nice they are on the outside! All cheats, and dominating, controlling masters at the end of the day. She was going to teach Ryder a lesson he was never going to forget. She was going to set him up and then hurt him like all men had hurt her. How incredibly stupid of her to have lost her senses momentarily and kissed him in the first place.

But when Ryder called a few hours later, she found that her feelings were a little more complicated.

"I just wanted to thank you for the lovely picnic," he said. "I feel like I don't want to brush my teeth for days, so I can keep the taste of you in my mouth."

"Perhaps you should consider shaving your teeth," she chuckled. "They'll get a bit furry after a few days without brushing."

Jinny caught herself in the middle of the flirty exchange. She felt the rage boil in her again. She would sort this man out. She was tired of men trying to dominate her all the time, tired of men cheating. She was going to learn all the tricks of the cheaters' trade! She needed to discover how they were all able to get away with cheating. She was going to make damn sure that by the time she was back in a long-term relationship, she would never be played or dominated by a man again.

***

RYDER CALLED HER the next day while she was at work.

"I want us to book a hotel room," he said.

She put on her controlled, seductive voice.

"Mmmm, that would be lovely. We can book a room, but I have a condition. You have to let me tie you up."

Ryder hesitated for a few seconds.

"Er, all right. So can I book a room for Thursday afternoon?"

Clearly he wanted to still be home in time for dinner.

"Yes, that sounds enticing."

On the inside she was thinking, OMG. I'm going to have him right where I want him. Boy, is he going to pay. But at the same time she felt sadness. She was about to lose a really nice, older guy friend. Men are just so disappointing.

By the time Thursday rolled around, she was well prepared.

She had bought the biggest, strongest pair of cable ties she could find, massage oil and a dildo. She had never been to a hotel room with a man who was not her husband, but she felt sure that the Holiday Inn would have a story to tell after she left Ryder there. The anger was helping her control her own fear - just enough to pull off her plan.

Ryder met her in the lobby. At reception he paid for the room in cash. He seemed anxious. He had these thin lips that became almost invisible when he was annoyed or anxious. She watched him carefully and put on her calm, in-control voice, as if she had done this a million times before. Jinny felt pleased that he was anxious, so he should be if he knew what was coming this afternoon! He wandered over to the bar and ordered two double whiskies to take with him to the room. He ordered her two Diet Cokes. He knew her well enough to know that she never touched alcohol.

He slid the card into the hotel-room door. The little light flashed green and he led her inside. Lights, camera, action, Jinny thought. Go big or go home! She entered the room as if she owned the place and threw her bags on the bed. Ryder walked up and grabbed her roughly around the waist, pulling her close to him. He kissed her hard on the mouth. She kissed him back just as hard, and his grip on her waist loosened. She kissed him again and then pushed him away.

"Get undressed and go shower."

Ryder did as he was told, thank God! Jinny started to sweat. Fuck, what had made her think she could pull off such an insane plan! Fuck was the operative word here! While Ryder was showering she got herself ready. She took out the cable ties and hid them under the bed. She put the dildo under the pillow, massage oil on the side table and laid fresh clean towels on the bed. Ryder emerged from the bathroom still shiny and wet with a towel around his waist. There it was again, that boyish look of his that she had come to enjoy so much. She needed to push those thoughts aside now. She had a job to do.

Jinny was wearing a tight black T-shirt without a bra, a beautiful Lola Luna open G-string and a black sarong.

Ryder grabbed his whisky and downed it like it was a glass of water, then he sauntered over and kissed her again as his towel fell to the floor. God, he was well hung. Pity. If he wasn't married she may have actually enjoyed him! She returned the kiss and pushed him into a sitting position on the bed. He sat with his hands over his dick and balls. She knelt and pushed his legs apart, coming to sit between his legs. She leaned forward as if she was going to suck his cock, teasing him as she slid her hand under the bed and found the cable ties.

"God Ryder, you've got such a beautiful, big cock."

She moved her hands up the inside of his leg, up his torso and down his arm and wrapped the cable tie around his wrist and tied it tight to the bedpost. In his face, was that a flicker of terror? He was nervous now; beads of sweat formed on his brow. Good. It was about time men knew what it was like to feel powerless and trapped.

Jinny left him on the bed and stepped back, so he could get a good look at her. He was desperate! She dropped her sarong to expose her lingerie, then slid back onto the bed, straddling him. She kissed his lips while lightly letting her labia slide over his dick. She was delighted to feel his instant erection.

"Lie on your tummy!"

She took another cable tie and lashed his other hand to the same bedpost. Now he felt himself losing control. And he didn't like it.

"What are you going to do to me?"

"Shh. You're not in charge today. I'm the boss. Now lie still!"

Jinny grabbed the massage oil from the side of the bed, slapped a splash onto her hands and began massaging his shoulders. He hated the feeling of oil on his body - he'd told her once and she had made a mental note of it. But this was dislike and pleasure at the same time. She wanted him to feel powerless and uncomfortable and turned on at the same time. She flipped him over and massaged his back, feeling him shift uncomfortably as his hard-on grew. It would be increasingly uncomfortable lying on it and being unable to adjust its position, with his hands cable-tied above his head.

Jinny kept up the rhythm of the massage. She removed her top and rubbed the oil over her breasts. Then she lowered herself over him and massaged his back with her breasts. He was moaning now, trying to twist his hands so he could flip over to connect with her. But he was going to have to beg. She ran her nipple across his ear, then pushed herself back, her pussy sliding down his spine. She scratched his back with the diamanté stone on her G-string. She lunged forward, ran her tongue around his ear and then plunged her tongue into his earhole. He was panting and moaning now, desperate to turn over.

"If you want to turn over, you'll have to beg me first."

She stuck her tongue down his ear again. He was breathing heavily, but laughing, in his deep, husky voice.

"Do you really want me to beg, Jinny?".

"Yes! Beg!"

She began to move her body again. She slid her pussy up and down his back, scratching him deeper with the diamanté as she rode him.

"Jinny," he moaned. It was like a deep, guttural, primordial growl.

"Please Jinny! Make love to me!"

She was surprised he hadn't said, fuck me! That's what all these Masters of the Universe said. They didn't want you to make love to them. They wanted you to fuck them, so they could fuck you back harder, and then throw you away like trash when they were finished with you. Why had he said make love to me?

"Turn over!"

His face was flushed. His dick was hard and throbbing now.

"Come and sit on me!"

There it was again. Even tied up, he was demanding things! She grabbed the dildo from under the pillow. As the twisting cable ties bit into his wrists, she knelt between his legs. She slid the dildo into her mouth and sucked it. She slid it between her breasts, still covered in massage oil. Then it was easy for her to ease the dildo between her vadge lips and into herself. She moaned and leaned back slightly as she pushed it deeper. He couldn't keep his eyes off her pussy and the dildo moving rhythmically in and out of her. Mesmerised as he was, he almost seemed in shock! Was he one of those traditional guys? A reader of Sex Manners For Men? Some older guys followed that book like a bible. His lovemaking was of that style, his instruction mode: lie down; take off your clothes; kiss me. He would probably never masturbate in front of her, but always make sure she came first!

If he was ever caught, he would use words like "I'm sorry, darling. It was nothing more than an indiscretion; it won't happen again." So old-fashioned. But he was twenty years older than her, after all

She changed position, sitting with her legs splayed. She started to play with her clit with one hand while sliding the dildo in and out of herself with the other. Then she pushed the dildo high up into herself and left it there. She slipped two fingers into her entrance.

Ryder started pulling on the cable ties, twisting his hands to try and get free, but she stayed just beyond his reach. She gasped, arching her back as she plunged the dildo in and out. In and out.

"How much do you want me, Ryder?"

His voice had become even lower, a desperate growl.

"I want you, Jinny. I want you to sit on me."

He was nearly where she wanted him. She removed the dildo and pulled him down the bed by the legs. She threw one of the towels over his erect dick, then sat down on him hard. His eyes had almost glazed over with lust.

"Please. I want to be inside you…"

He was thrusting his dick up towards her. He was ready.

Now she was going to hop off and leave him turned on and vulnerable, tied to the bed. She was going to get dressed and leave and never contact him or have anything to do with him again.

She was going to let him suck her breast and dangle her vadge just out of reach of his lips, and then she was going to leave him. How was he going to get himself out of this bind? How would he explain to his wife why he was late? She was going to leave the hotel door open, so his shouts for help would be heard. She didn't want to have to worry that he'd be tied to the bed for days, in his own filth, till he dehydrated and died in the bed. She didn't want to kill him or take away his dignity. She just wanted to teach him a lesson. But who knew who would eventually come to his aid and find him like this?

She moved forward on his body, to let him suck her breast. He latched onto her like a baby. Oh, she loved her breasts being sucked. It made her tingle all over. But she quickly pulled away. She sat on his stomach just above his hard cock. She ran her hands up his side, stopping at his cable-tied wrists. Then she bent forward and looked him straight in the eyes. Their noses were nearly touching. She remained completely still; she just looked at him. Ryder returned her gaze, and for the first time she saw who he really was. She could see his vulnerability. He was just a boy who wanted to be wanted and loved. He was probably as lonely and sad as she was. He spoke in that soft, husky voice, his eyes welling up.

"Jinny."

"Yes, Ryder?"

"I've never allowed anyone to tie me up before. I don't know why I agreed to do this. It's just… There's something about you that makes me feel less weary and sad."

She pulled back. Shit, she hadn't planned on this. He was an arrogant, cheating arse, whom she wanted to teach a lesson. Now he'd learned what it was like to feel dominated and vulnerable and under the control of someone else. Here he was, helpless. Damn it to hell! There was no way she could leave him tied to the bed. She wasn't that malicious. She'd just wanted to teach him a lesson. He'd jolly well learned it already!

"Well, Ryder, she said. "Now you know what it's like to be dominated and vulnerable for once."

She slid off the bed, walked to the bathroom and had a shower. When she was done, she dressed, then came back into the bedroom and packed away the massage oil and the dildo. She stood by the bed. Ryder lay tied to the bed with the towel over his groin. He was soft now, and wild-eyed.

"You're not going to leave me like this, are you?"

Without a word, she reached into her bag and took out a pair of scissors.

"I have to go, Ryder. You got off lightly today."

She cut him loose. As the ties gave way he cried out, and recoiled instinctively. She turned away from the bed before he could recover; she closed the door behind her. As she walked down the corridor, she thought she heard gasps and mutterings. He was going to need a few stiff whiskies to get over that!

***

JINNY DID NOT feel vindicated, or pleased with her afternoon's handiwork. She just felt cheap, sad and ashamed of herself. She had wanted to prove to herself that all men were self-centred, dominating cheats, who cared nothing for the women they used and hurt along the way. But she'd seen a sweet, vulnerable side to Ryder that she could not discount. Or even quite understand.

She decided not to see him again. What was she thinking anyway! Trying to teach him a lesson! As if men ever learned from anything they did! Why was she behaving like this anyway? She missed the kids, and the lunches with Ryder had eased the pain of her disastrous marriage. Ryder helped her forget that longing for her kids. Now she'd stuffed that up well and truly too. She needed to focus on her work, to get her life back on track. She didn't need the complication of a married man in her life now too!

The counselling side of her work had slowed down, though. She wondered if it was because word had got out about her collapsed marriage. Or was she being punished by God for her disciplining of Ryder? She'd have felt no guilt about her dalliance with Ryder if he'd been single. But he was married. Now that righteous anger seemed to have disappeared and waves of guilt washed over her.

Ryder had tried to contact her a few times and Jinny had been pleasant enough, but she'd lied that she had flown back to the Cape to be with the kids for a while. She didn't want to see him or face him again. She wanted him to go away and leave her alone. He was just another disappointing, cheating husband with a bit of a sweet side. In truth, she was more disappointed in her own behaviour than she was in him. She knew better, she counselled people and worked with this kind of thing all the time. Why the hell did she get involved in something so incredibly stupid in the first place?

Work dwindled even further over the next few months and Jinny started to worry. Finally, one of the websites she used to advertise her counselling work called up. They wanted to see her medical board registration. She asked why now? She had been advertising on their site for years. They gave a weak answer about checking up on all of their counsellors' registrations. They were going to take her information off their site until she forwarded them her medical certification.

The call was odd, and it stunk of the estranged ex. This was the third site that had suddenly stopped carrying her ads. It was worrying, as these sites were the best advertising tool she had. How was she going to get her life back on track and look after the kids, if she couldn't work!

She had a bad feeling that Justin and Nora were trying to sabotage her work. Perhaps they'd lodged some fraudulent complaint with the medical board. But since no one would be up front about what was going on, she had no way to respond. Even if they had complained to the medical board, it shouldn't make a difference as she was registered with the counselling board. Not the medical board! Something was out of whack, but at the end of the day she wasn't getting as many patients as she needed, to stay afloat.

Ryder had sent her a few WhatsApp messages asking to see her again, but she really didn't want to see him. She felt guilty and ashamed about what she'd done and yet thrilled and disturbed that she'd been capable of sex like that. She really just wanted him to go away. Eventually, she sent him a rather spiteful email, advising that she really couldn't be involved with a married man. But in the event that he was looking for someone to shag she could refer him to a few excellent brothels or furnish him with a list of married ladies looking for something discreet on the side!

That should shut him up and make him go away. She felt a bit melancholy as she pressed send on her email. She'd enjoyed Ryder's company and there was something about him that made her feel grounded. He'd felt like a lighthouse in a wild storm, a stable point of reference in a world that was spinning out of control.

***

THE NEXT JO'BURG phase was surreal. Jinny loved her work helping people get through their personal issues; stabilising their lives and relationships. And yet her personal life was an absolute mess. She was squatting on Carol's couch and she hadn't seen her kids in months because she couldn't afford air tickets. Besides that, she was being summonsed again and couldn't even afford an attorney. To make matters worse, because she earned more than R3 000 a month, she didn't qualify for Legal Aid. Jinny had even been to see the professor of the Wits Law Clinic but he'd also politely declined to assist her. He said his young candidate attorneys were not experienced enough to deal with such a "vicious, voluminous and vexatious" legal matter. She was at the end of her tether. It felt like she was on a defibrillator half the time – shaky and anxious. It was like she was lying on a cold mortuary slab with someone stabbing and twisting a steak knife in her heart, then standing back and laughing at their handiwork. As soon as she felt she'd caught her breath and got over the pain of the last onslaught, it would happen again.

She didn't trust anyone enough to talk about what was going on. She couldn't talk to her work colleagues, friends or even her family. As supportive as her family were, she didn't trust her mother's or her stepfather's advice. She and her mom had an ambivalent relationship – as much as her mom probably loved her, she didn't like her. Jinny didn't trust her advice because ultimately her mother had never really understood her.

Her emotions teetered between overwhelming feelings of betrayal, desperation and loneliness and then wild, volcanic anger and rage at the unkindness, injustice and dishonesty of men.

She couldn't sleep at night, so she read. Then she was so tired during the day that she was basically sleepwalking. She had started sweating uncontrollably at night, and now during the day too. She was going through at least three changes of clothes a day. Shit, she thought, just her luck to start going through menopause now, in the middle of this whole mess. Surely she was too young to be starting menopause at 36?

Jinny knew she was on the edge of a canyon, but she was not going to jump in because her kids believed in her. Her kids believed she could sort this out. And it was knowing that her kids had faith in her that kept her going.

Despite herself, she was also missing Ryder. It was three months since she had seen or spoken to him. That last email had clearly done the trick. But she missed his husky voice and that explosive laugh that just erupted out of him… She missed his strong, steady grip, holding her hand when she felt distressed. As a rule, she didn't like people touching her, but she liked him holding her hand. It made her feel safe. Why had she been so stupid as to kiss him in the first place! That was what had ruined the friendship. Those hotel room antics were just the final nail in the coffin. All men were the same, Jinny thought to herself – desperately disappointing in the end!

A year after moving out of the house she'd shared with Justin, Jinny was still trapped by him. She couldn't date anyone because she was still married. She wasn't getting any maintenance money for the kids because she couldn't afford an attorney. She knew Justin wasn't going to give up being malicious any time soon. It was only a question of time before she learned what more he had in store for her. Work was dwindling. She missed the kids like mad, and she was as destitute as she'd ever been. But no matter how bad it got, she knew she could never have stayed with Justin for one more day.

She had always been faithful to Justin. She wanted her marriage to work. Who wants to be a destitute single mom with two small kids anyway! It's much easier to cry in a Porsche than to be left on the porch! All she'd ever wanted was to be loved, and to be happy in her marriage. But now she'd been tarnished, tarred and feathered as some kind of a lewd porn star, an unfaithful slut. Fuck you, Justin, she thought. I was a good wife to you. I don't deserve what you've dished out.

Jinny had been widowed prior to marrying Justin. She'd married Dylan, her first love, when she was just 21. He was ten years older than her, and of Irish and Afrikaans descent, with a mop of thick, wild, curly brown hair. Dylan wasn't exactly good looking, but he was funny and he had a way of teasing and making her laugh that she had loved. Dylan was in bush reconnaissance and as calm and easy-going as he was on the outside, there was a cold-blooded killer on the inside. But Jinny never saw that cold-blooded side. They never spoke about his work, but it must have been responsible for his suicide. She never really got over him shooting himself and leaving her alone. She was 26.

Just before she lost Dylan, she'd worked at an insurance company with Christiaan. They'd been work colleagues and friends. Christiaan was 37 and had been in an army unit with Dylan in the apartheid days. Although he never spoke about the army, he clearly had a bond with Dylan too. He was there for her when Dylan died – whether out of friendship, or some sense of duty to Dylan, she never worked out. But still, she felt Chris understood her.

When Justin came along, he was jealous of her friendship with Chris and had made it unpleasant and difficult for her to see him. But she had retained her friendship with Chris quietly on the side because he was a link to her past life with Dylan.

Chris was half Scottish and half Afrikaans (a bit like Dylan). He was tall and slender, with a gorgeous physique. He always smelled good, looked good… the kind of body you could lick tequila shots off! Like Jinny, Chris had married young – a beautiful woman who was a great mom, but who had become a bit of a fat, disinterested blob. And Chris had always been a women worshipper.

He'd told her how he idolised women – with a particular reverence for the workings of their vaginas. Chris was both a slut and a romantic at heart. He never wanted to conquer women, he just wanted to pleasure and please them. Ultimately, he enjoyed the thrill of thrusting his cock into a new women and bringing her to orgasm. He was a bit of a male whore, there was no getting away from that. Jinny had always known this about him and he had often teased her, saying she was one of the few women he really respected. It was because, as long as they had known each other, and no matter how much he had charmed her, he had never been able to get into her pants. Now, ironic as all hell, Justin was accusing Chris of being Skyla's father! That's who he'd mentioned in his lawyer's letter! God! Jinny wished Chris had been Skyla's father. Even if Chris was a women eater he was a great dad.

Now Jinny really wanted to see Chris. She felt she was drifting. She needed to see and speak to someone who had known her before. Before Justin, before the counselling practice took off, before the kids, before it all had gone up in flames. She wanted to speak to someone who wouldn't judge her. Someone who knew of the heartache she'd gone through losing her first husband, but who knew nothing about the assaults, degradation and humiliation that she had suffered at the hands of Justin.

After the army, Chris had carved out a successful career in financial IT. Now he was one of the well-dressed suits, an acclaimed company director with a few degrees to his name. In a far sexier, more suave package, but with the same penchant for disrobing and uncovering the mystical pleasures of the vagina. His titles and degrees may have changed, but Jinny knew that under that suit was the same person. Chris never changed and that was something reassuring. Jinny needed to see him.

She arranged to meet Chris for tea at a restaurant near her work. It was a pleasant tea, a great blast from the past. They both laughed and did some catching up. Jinny told him that she'd left Justin a year ago, that the kids were with her folks in the Cape, and that she was still trying to piece her life together. Oh, and he was being accused of being Skyla's father! Ha, ha! How they laughed at that! Just talking to Chris about what was happening made the whole situation therapeutic. Sure when you said out loud that you were living on someone's couch, it seemed dire and hopeless, but Chris – just like Dylan – had a way of making her relax and laugh. At one point he leaned over the table, and took both her hands in his.

"Jinny," he said.

"What?"

"I would be proud to have Skyla as my daughter. She is a beautiful little girl and she really deserves to have a good daddy. And since I have been accused of being her father, can I at least have one kiss from you?"

Jinny thought- what the heck! After all, they were both still married. And it's only a kiss. She stretched across the table and kissed him. It was a gentle kiss on the lips, but immediately the energy between them surged. Something suddenly changed. Jinny pulled away and stood up.

"I have to be going," she said. "I have an appointment."

"Okay," he said. "Let's leave together."

She was quite shaken by the unexpected intensity of the kiss. But he was calm as he smiled his gentle smile. He probably enjoys watching me get into a spin, Jinny thought to herself. She grabbed her bag and leaped up, knocking over the teacup as she swung her bag onto her shoulder.

"Oh, shit. Sorry!"

She tried to rush out of the restaurant, but he was right next to her. He gently slipped his hand into hers, interlocking their fingers.

"Jinny, darling, it's okay."

He led her calmly and gently out of the restaurant. They took an elevator down to the underground basement where her car was parked.

There was no one else in the lift and as the doors closed, Chris grabbed her other hand and pushed her up against the side of the elevator. He kissed her gently on the lips again. He tasted like candy and he felt so divine pushing up close to her body. She immediately felt her pussy lubricating. He pulled back and she leaned into him again, finding and claiming his mouth. He responded with a stronger kiss, sliding his hands onto her bum and pulling her closer. Then his hands were up inside her bra, circling and squeezing her nipples. She let out a moan and arched her body into him. The door of the elevator slid open and he calmly slipped his hands from her shirt. He took her hand again and led her to the car. Jinny felt almost dishevelled as she dug in her bag for her keys, then fumbled to open the door. As she opened the car door, Chris swung her around and pushed her up against the vehicle, devouring her with another ravenous kiss as he opened the car door with his free right hand. Then he gently pushed her inside.

"Goodbye, Jinny," he gasped.

From where she sat, his hard dick was bulging in his pants at eye level.

"You're so good, Jinny," he said.

"You're such a slut," she grinned.

"I've been waiting for you a long time, Jinny."

Then he stepped away from the car door and she drove off.

Wow! That was unexpected, but hell it felt good! She'd felt alive and connected to someone for the first time in years! Even if it was only for a few seconds. The alleged father of her daughter!

Her heart pounded in her chest. She was panting like she'd just got off a treadmill as she slipped her parking ticket in at the boom exit. And that was only a kiss! No wonder he had so many women begging to shag him! She would have to stay away from Chris, because with moves like his, she knew she wanted more. But she wasn't going to stand in line to be shagged by him.

Once the adrenalin had worn off, the old feelings of drifting and loneliness and missing her kids gnawed at her soul. She was now a confirmed insomniac, sweating and anxious all the time. The hopelessness descended on her life again. Financially, she had no idea how she was going to survive another month.

She spoke to Luke and Skyla every day, reassuring them that she would be home soon and that she was never going to leave them again. But it had already been six months since she'd last seen them. The kids had settled in well with her parents and at school, and their days seemed busy and happy. She was relieved that they were safe, relaxed and doing well, but it was starting to feel like even they might slip away from her.

Luke seemed especially relaxed and happy with her parents. Skyla was the opposite, asking about her all the time.

"Mommy, when are you coming to fetch me?"

***

IT WAS A Tuesday. The Wednesday would be National Women's Day. On Friday she would be flying home to see the kids. Her folks had taken pity on all concerned and paid for a return ticket for her. She was so looking forward to seeing their little faces. Skype and mobile could only take you so far. She wanted to hold the kids and hug them and chat to them and snuggle on the couch, cook for them, organise their cupboards for them and hear all about their school friends. So much to catch up on!

Jinny generally woke up exhausted, but she forced herself through the day. She willed herself to get up, to get dressed, to put a smile on her face and to focus on what she needed to get out of this mess. It was no use wallowing in the pain of everything she'd lost because, Lord knows, she had lost all her material possessions. Jinny kept telling herself to focus on getting out of this mess – not on her material losses.

She feared poverty. It had something to do with her parents telling her as a little girl that if she didn't work hard at school, she would land up like one of those hobos on the streets. Or maybe it was just that hobos in general frightened her. She knew she was getting close to this point, and it was only by the grace of God that she was sleeping on a friend's couch and not in a backyard shack in Triomf.

Jinny had had a privileged childhood. She had been adopted aged three by a rich, liberal, anti-apartheid family. Her childhood was rather wild and negligent. Her parents threw a lot of parties, attended political meetings and Jinny had grown up in a huge home with several housekeepers. There was a white, English nanny from the UK to oversee the staff and drive her around, and she had attended private schools with her siblings. Daddy had a six-seater Cirrus light aeroplane and they would frequently fly off on holiday to wild, African locations. Daddy fancied himself quite a pilot but would frequently get lost. This was way before the time of GPS and the control tower would usually have to talk him down. Whenever this happened, Mummy would go extra white in the face, hanging onto the edge of her seat and looking for beacons, trying to help Daddy to land the plane. Mummy hated flying with Daddy, but Jinny quite enjoyed the extra hours of circling around in the air. Daddy always said that if the worst came to the worst he could land on the road, so Jinny could never understand what Mummy was so worried about, apart from it being problematic if they ran out of fuel and had to glide for a while.

These were her fondest childhood memories, but not everything was as jolly hockey sticks as that. Daddy had started touching her when she was ten. At first Jinny had pushed away and resisted, but Daddy told her that Mummy masturbated all the time and that when little girls started growing up it was okay for their Daddies to touch them. It was all part of growing up. Jinny had fought and resisted at first, but Mummy was a journalist involved in the struggle and fighting for people's rights, so she was away a lot. Daddy said he did this to Mummy too, so Jinny thought it this was just something that Daddies did. But still, she didn't like it.

Jinny tried locking her door, but Daddy took the key away. Then she tried hiding under the bed, but Daddy pulled her out from under the bed by her ankle and took her to his room. Then he put her in the bed and pulled her panties to the side. When he did that, she tried to lock her legs together, but he was too strong for her. He gripped her arms and put them above her head. Then he held them tight with one hand. He used his other hand to open her legs. He kept them open by putting his heavy leg over her legs. The more she fought, the more he held her down. She felt like those pieces of meat she'd seen hanging on the hooks at the butcher. He told her to shhhhhhhhhh. Then he would shove his big fingers into her privates even harder.

Daddy was 45 and he seemed huge. He was 6'2" with an athletic build and big muscles. He was very sporty and played golf and tennis every week. Their home over-looked the country club and Daddy was always on the golf course or on the tennis court at home. She would scream in pain and beg him to let her go. She'd try to wiggle away, but he would hold her down and tell her to shhhhhhhhhh. Then he shoved his big fingers deeper into her. He had skew teeth that overlapped in the front, and while he was tearing at the inside of her little body, all she could see was his horrible teeth. And the spit spraying on her face as he kept saying over and over shhhhhhhhhhhh, shhhhhh-hhhhh, shhhhhhhhhhhh. And the overwhelming smell of Brut cologne.

How apt that he'd worn Brut. That's what he was. Nothing but a brute, hiding behind his money, his good Natal English accent, good family from the right side of the tracks and private school education. Jinny could feel the inside of her body tearing and it felt like someone had taken a red hot poker and shoved it up her privates. But the more she whimpered and cried, the more he would carry on until she stopped fight-ing and then he would let her go and say, "There now, that wasn't so bad now was it? Daddy's going to turn you into a real woman."

Jinny's legs would be shaking and she would stagger off to the bathroom, where she'd sit on the toilet, bleeding. She'd feel like she needed to wee, but it hurt so much to wee. She would sit on the toilet for ages, whimpering quietly, forcing herself not to cry too loudly in case he came back for her again. She wasn't sure how babies were made, but she had seen horses mating and it seemed a bit like what Daddy was doing. It had something to do with mating, but she wasn't sure because he was touching her privates. He never tried to mount her like the horses did, so maybe this was just something that Daddies did to turn you into a woman. If this was what being a woman was all about, Jinny wasn't sure she wanted to be one!

After the searing pain and burning would come days of itching and burning. Jinny had learned that as soon as Mummy went out and the housekeepers were sent to their rooms, then Daddy would come for her. The only way to get away was to climb up onto the wall and then up onto the roof of their three-storey home and to wait for Mummy to come home late at night. On the days when Jinny couldn't get away in time, she had learned to keep still and quiet and to let him do whatever he wanted to her body. That way he would let her go sooner.

"You see, Jinny? Now that you've stopped fighting me, it's not so bad, is it? I think you're getting used to me playing with you now. I love you, Jinny. Daddy's going to turn you into a real woman…"

By the time she was 11, Jinny had stopped feeling love for anyone. But she never told anyone, because Daddy had told her to shhhhhh.

Jinny knew this was the reason she had wanted to become a sexologist. She wanted to be able to help other women who had been through the same thing. South Africa had an insanely high abuse rate, with more than two out of every three children being molested before the age of 14. Almost half of child rape victims were children under the age of three! As dramatic and horrific as rape was, everyone was so fascinated by the abomination and the morbid horror of rape that few people ever stopped to think what happened to the victims after the rape. Were they ever able to recover and get into functional relationships? How was anyone ever able to make any sense of an episode that seemed so surreal and out of context with the rest of their lives? Jinny felt that she was still one of the lucky ones. She had survived. She'd been given a decent education and she'd trained in a field where she could do some good. She wanted to make a difference to other women's lives and she had. It made her feel better that what she had gone through was not all for nothing. She'd turned the experience into something positive. But though she'd helped countless people, she'd still never been able to speak out and admit that it had happened to her too.

Jinny had learned that the high life came with its own set of rules and a sense of entitlement and ownership. It was something she despised, but she was sure that poverty came with its own massive challenges. And now Jinny was getting to face poverty square in the face. During hard times, what was the difference between someone scraping themselves off the floor and succeeding - or landing up on the street?

Once, on a flight from Durban after a rugby match, Jinny had sat next to the father of a Springbok rugby player. He told Jinny a story about his brother. He had been a successful anaesthetist who had suffered from clinical depression. He had eventually left the medical field and landed up as a hobo on the street. His brother, desperate to help his sibling, had taken him into his home, but his brother had still landed up back on the street. Finally, he had paid for his brother to live in a tiny cottage on a farm, away from the desperation of the city. At first he'd seemed happy, but within a few months, he was found dead, hanging from a tree outside his little shack.

She'd heard many similar stories. Her friend Shaz – a successful businesswoman – had a father who was living in a white squatter camp outside Krugersdorp. She said he seemed happier living in a squatter camp than in what was considered normal society.

Rock bottom was never that far off – even for professional people with degrees. What stood between her and the street? Not a hell of a lot – she already felt like a hobo living out of a suitcase, on her friend's couch.

***

JINNY ASKED SHAZ to take her to visit the camp. She wanted to see for herself what being a white squatter was all about. She was appalled at the idea of going, but she wanted to face the reality, and perhaps overcome her terror of being poor.

She'd arranged to go with Shaz on a Tuesday. That morning she popped by her office to pick up a client's file. She was surprised to recognise her old friend Anton – the sheriff of the court – at reception.

"Sheriff," she said. "Are you here for me again or is someone else in trouble this time?"

"Jinny! I'm sorry, but it's you I've come to serve papers on!"

Oh God. She sighed and invited him through to their tea area. She grabbed herself a cup of tea and as she sat down, he handed her another huge wad of papers. Again that familiar icy dread washed over her. She felt like she was back on that mortuary slab. The document was an urgent high court application for custody of Skyla. Jinny looked up at Anton with her bottom lip quivering.

"I don't have any legal representation, and this is a massive, complicated affidavit I need to respond to. Today is Tuesday. Wednesday and Thursday are public holidays and I'm due to appear in court on Friday... How am I..."

"You're right. It's hard. I'm sorry to be the bearer of bad news."

He must have used those words a thousand times. He stood up and left.

Jinny pushed the affidavit into her briefcase, and went to reception to wait for Shaz. There was no point in cancelling her trip. There was nothing she could do about replying to this affidavit right now – she was too stressed to even think. She would have to address the problem later in the day.

Jinny was surprised by what she found at the camp. She had expected abject poverty and squalor. But many of the squatters had electricity, beds and fridges in their shacks. Running water and bathroom amenities were a problem, though. They had three long-drop toilets and four showers for 200 people. The kids didn't go to school and there were no jungle gyms or play equipment for them. They played in the sand, running around filthy and bare bottomed. The residents were suspicious and unwelcoming. They went inside and shut their doors when they walked by.

But the only difference between her and the people here was she had hope and determination! The people in the camp had given up on life. They were basically waiting hopelessly for life to dish them out another bad hand or for death to arrive. She realised that, however bad her situation was, that was not her! She had hope! She had determination! With the rest of her life ahead of her, and two beautiful children to live for, there was no way she was giving up!

Jinny couldn't wait to get out of the squatter camp. She felt grateful to have found the answer to her question. She had the winning formula already. She just had to keep on going! Focus on what you need, she told herself. Not what you've lost! Keep on going! Be grateful every single day for what you have because it could be way worse!

***

IT WAS ANOTHER Tuesday evening. Jinny had two days to respond to the 80-page affidavit. She needed to outline why she should be the bona fide primary caregiver and why Justin should only see Luke and Skyla under supervision.

What the hell did she know about writing replying affidavits! Frankly, she knew nothing. She was no attorney, she was a counsellor. But she needed to protect Luke and Skyla from an abusive parent. She was hardly enamoured with the idea of their being exposed to Justin again, but he was their father and it was their right to see their father if they wanted to. She just needed to make sure the kids were safe and that what they wanted was adhered to. But this concept of putting the child's rights first had never been put before the high court. There was still no precedent in South African law. South Africa's government departments ran big, anti-child-abuse campaigns about having zero tolerance for abuse, but in fact there were loopholes in the law. For example, a child could have a permanent protection order in place against an abusive parent, but the parent could still exercise his or her right to see the child under supervision. Even if the parent had been convicted of abusing the child! The law had recently been changed so that the rights of the child were paramount, to assert that it was the right of the child to see the parent not the right of the parent to see the child. This was a huge breakthrough in children's rights, but a case of this nature had still not been heard. No precedent had been set and Jinny was no lawyer!

Justin was again trying to imply that Jinny was some kind of prostitute porn star, who had falsely represented herself to the medical and dental council as a psychologist. Meanwhile she was a counsellor! He had included in his annexures a letter of complaint that Nora had submitted to the medical council, as well as a letter of complaint on a medical council letterhead that she had emailed to the websites Jinny advertised on. She had known it all along! The two of them were sabotaging her business. It wasn't enough that she had lost her home and all her material possessions. Now they were trying to make it impossible for her to support the children. What they were doing made no logical sense. Surely you'd want your ex-wife to be financially stable and thriving in business? That way you would not have to support her or the children financially! But hatred, jealousy and greed were emotions that never made sense. Justin was so filled with hatred and set on revenge, on bringing Jinny to her knees, that he would stop at nothing.

Today, Jinny felt rejuvenated with a new appreciation for her own powers of hope and determination. She was determined to be better – and Skyla and Luke's safety and well-being were on the line. So come hell or high water she was going to type up point-by-point responses to this bloody affidavit. She had to do it herself, because even if she could have appointed an attorney today, Wednesday and Thursday were public holidays and the application was going to be heard on Friday. So by hook or by crook, Jinny was going to be standing in front of the judge on Friday representing herself and doing the best she could.

The sum total of her legal experience was a couple of desperate sobbing appearances in court, and watching Judge Judy on TV. But that would just have to be enough for now. Perhaps she should have watched more Bear Grylls as well. Some survival tips would be handy right now.

There was no time for a lawyer, but Jinny realised she needed help. She'd have to call in the troops. She put in mercy calls to three of her old school friends – Lesedi, Deánne and Eva. These days Lesedi was an architect and a director of a construction company, Deánne was a specialist vet and Eva was studying to be an attorney. The three of them had a few things in common – they had experience in writing and trawling through pages of documentation and they were all her friends. Jinny knew they would help in a real emergency. And this was one!

They convened at Lesedi's house and planned their attack. They divided the 80-page affidavit into three roughly equal parts. Jinny would type out a response to each allegation, then the three of them would rewrite her replies into a reasonably legal and objective tone. The four of them worked solidly from Tuesday evening through to Thursday evening to get that affidavit together. God alone knows how they managed to pull it off, but they did.

The manic process left her frazzled, but she really started appreciating her girlfriends. She wasn't all alone after all. These amazing women had rallied around her to work through the night – twice – to help her keep her children.

Jinny woke at 4am on Friday feeling hammered. She didn't sleep well as a rule, but now she'd hardly slept since Tuesday evening. She felt exhausted, hung over and highly irritable. It was like the world had gone into slow motion, but her thoughts had speeded up! It was stress, stratospheric emotional stress. But bugger it. She would just have to gather what wits she still had about her and face her estranged ex and his girlfriend with their entourage of attorneys like a pack of baying hell-hounds.

Attorneys and advocates are creatures of instruction. When you have someone paying you hundreds of thousands to represent them in high court, why would you worry about what's in the best interests of the estranged wife and children! Ultimately, the only thing they worry about is the best interests of their bank accounts.

Jinny had a feeling of impending doom. She was back on the mortuary slab. The knife was being twisted again. She shook like a leaf and the sweats were uncontrollable.

But today was not about how she felt, or what they were going to do to her. Today was about the kids. She was going to go in there, handle herself with dignity and grace and do her damnedest to protect her kids. So put on your big-girl panties, she told herself. Put on three pairs of big-girl panties if you need to, get your arse to the high court, and do what you need to do.

Jinny was going to go to the high court on her own. She didn't want to expose her friends to Justin's harassment and intimidation as had happened with Nellie. She wore a black, full-length skirt, a black long-sleeved top and black shoes. She sprayed her hair down into place. Shows like Suits on TV made attorneys out to be such a well-dressed, suave bunch, all rushing around looking important and busy. But the Johannesburg High Court was not an American TV show. The place was dirty and run down, with faulty elevators and lawyers looking like they had they not slept for days and they hadn't bathed either. It was easy enough for them to get away with it, though. Those long black court robes could hide a world of filth. High court is not a court of emotion, it's a court of law. It's a dirty, cold and uncaring place, where you are only as strong as the paper in front of you.

Jinny knew the Urgent Court rooms were on the sixth floor. She'd been there before with her attorney – back in the days when she had been able to afford legal representation.

She arrived at court at 8am and sat on a bench at the very back of the room, in the right-hand corner up against the wall. She was the first and only person in the courtroom. She watched the clerk of the court walk in and take his position. She didn't know his name, but she recognised him from the last time. As far as judges go, she knew that the Urgent application judges were rotated, so you never knew which judge you were going to get. They didn't wear name tags, so it was impossible to even know the name of the judge she was going to address.

The clerk acknowledged her with a nod, and Jinny did the same. Part of her was scared rigid, but that was okay. She was here and she was going to do her best to represent her kids' case.

The courtroom filled up. Justin entered with Nora and his attorney Dimwit, and two advocates. They all seemed quite jovial as they scanned the courtroom. Jinny wanted to sink into the corner so that they wouldn't recognise her. She was all alone. She was going to try to defend the kids, but just being in his presence brought back the sickening fear of having to defend herself physically if Justin attacked her.

"All rise!"

Everyone stood as the judge entered, then they all sat as he took his seat.

The clerk began reading out cases.

"Engelbrecht vs Engelbrecht."

Two sets of attorneys came forward. They took turns stating their case to the judge. He then made a decision, read out his ruling, smacked his mallet down on a circular block and the case was over.

Justin, Nora, Dimwit and their advocates were sitting two benches in front of Jinny and she could hear them talking and laughing between themselves. Justin was almost sniggering as he turned to Dimwit and said, "I knew she wouldn't be here today. She doesn't have any legal representation and she would not have had time to get any. Even if she did pitch up today she would not have been able to respond to our affidavit in time. She's so dumb she probably did not know what half of the Latin words meant anyway." Sniggers all round.

Jinny had to admit that the Latin words had been challenging, but Google is a magical thing. Who needs to be smart when you have Google! They were still going to have to put *vigilantibus non dormientibus aequitas subvenit* in their pipe and smoke it by the time they were finished dragging her through the courts!

"Number 40. Pringle (Gent) vs Pringle."

Jinny froze. The clerk called the case again.

"Number 40. Pringle (Gent) vs Pringle!"

Dimwit and his attorney stepped forward.

"I'm sorry, your honour, but it seems Mrs Pringle… Gent…. Er, Pringle-Gent. She was unable to make court today." Jinny saw the clerk of the court lean over the podium to speak to the judge. The Judge called out.

"Mrs Pringle-Gent, if you are here today, please come forward."

Jinny stood up. Her hands shook; there was a roaring in her ears. On shaky legs she walked down the aisle of the courtroom and stood in front of the judge.

"Yes your lordship," Jinny said. "I am here."

The judge asked if she had legal representation. She said she had none, and that she was here to represent herself today.

The judge asked Jinny if she had replied to the affidavit and Jinny confirmed that she had. She handed a copy of the answering affidavit to the clerk.

Dimwit's attorney moved forward.

"My lord, I must register a complaint. I have received no copy of the answering affidavit."

The judge leaned forward.

"I must remind counsel that the rules of the Urgent Court are not the same as High Court. In an Urgent Court application it is not necessary for the defendant to supply the plaintiff with a copy of the answering affidavit timeously. I will, however, require a 45-minute recess to read the replying affidavit.

"All rise."

Recess over. The judge entered. He was Judge Stander , she had learned in the interim. Again everyone stood briefly.

"Mrs Pringle-Gent, do you agree that this is an urgent matter?"

"Your honour, er… Your worship, I do not. I have been the bona fide primary care giver of the children for 18 months now. Mr Pringle has alleged that the child in question is not his and has demanded paternity tests. On the one hand, he wants custody but in other affidavits he wants to absolve himself of all responsibility for the children. Besides all of that, the children are happy and are being well taken care of."

The judge looked at Jinny with sad eyes. He realised she had no clue how to address a High Court judge. Jinny felt small, stupid and ashamed that she didn't know what she was doing. The judge said something in Latin and then smacked his mallet down again. He must have given a ruling, but she had not heard it, nor did she have any clue what it meant.

"Excuse me, your honour," said Jinny. "I didn't hear what you said. Please may I ask you to repeat it so I can write it down?"

Judge Stander looked down his nose at her and took a deep breath.

"Mrs Pringle-Gent, I am a High Court judge, not a secretary. You are welcome to get the transcript of my judgement."

Jinny didn't know what a transcript was, nor where she should go to get one. But she'd have to find out quickly. As she turned to leave the courtroom, she heard Justin and Nora, Dimwit and their advocates burst out laughing.

Jinny felt so small and so stupid, so humiliated! But they could have thrown eggs or grenades at her, she would still have come here to protect her children. Had she managed that? She still didn't know what the ruling was.

"Silence in court," the judge roared. "There will be no laughing in my court."

He looked at Justin.

"Mr Pringle," he said. "Your wife wants a divorce. Life happens and change happens. I suggest you learn to deal with it. You are abusing the Urgent Court system. You are banned from using Urgent Court again and the only time that you will be allowed back into High Court is to divorce your wife."

With that he smacked his mallet down again.

"Please leave my courtroom immediately, Mr Pringle!"

Jinny just stood dumbstruck, staring at the judge. She looked across at Justin and his pack from hell stomping out of the courtroom and burst into tears. She still didn't know what the judge had said about the children! Surely this was a good sign, though. It was all getting a bit much. She didn't know how much more of this she could take. She clung to the back of a bench to steady herself. The clerk of the court came across.

"Can I assist you, ma'am?"

Jinny nodded and the clerk helped her out of the court room. Tears were streaming down her face and she was in such a state that she didn't care.

"I made a real fool of myself in there didn't I?"

"No," said the clerk of the court. "I thought you were incredibly brave to represent yourself when you had no idea what you were doing. But you seemed determined to protect your children."

Jinny wasn't sure she'd heard the clerk correctly. Did he say she was brave? She'd thought she was just stupid!

"Sir?" Jinny asked. "I don't know your name and I don't know what the clerk of the court even does. Could you please explain to me in English what the judgement was?"

The clerk looked at her and smiled gently.

"Mrs Pringle (Gent), the judge threw the matter out of Urgent Court. He ruled that the matter was not urgent, and no orders were put in place. That means you are free to go and the children are still in your care."

OMG. OMG. OMG. The kids were safe! With that, the dam wall broke. The tears kept rolling down her face. But somewhere inside her emotions were flooding her synapses. She was so relieved at having saved her family. Exhilarated at winning her case, but more than anything, just shattered, exhausted. The clerk of the court reached into his gown and handed her a tissue.

"Thank you, sir," she sobbed, then turned and wandered out of the courtroom.

OM freaking G, Jinny thought. The four of them – Lesedi, Deánne, Eva and she herself – had managed to keep the kids safe. God had been merciful and gracious and delivered the kids back into her care!

***

IT HAD BEEN nearly a year since Jinny had seen or spoken to Ryder, though she still thought about him. There was no way she was going to call him, though.

Some things were slow to change. Jinny was in her office stressing about her lack of income, trying to plan a new marketing campaign now that Justin and Nora had alienated all her media contacts. Then Ryder called.

"Jinny," he said. "I've been out to tea with all the girls you put me in touch with. I haven't contacted any of the brothels – that's not for me. But it's really you that I want to take out for tea."

Jinny laughed. It was lovely to hear Ryder's bear growl of a voice again, and he did have a lovely way with words.

"Ryder! Did you really go out to tea with all those girls?"

Ryder just laughed, "…and now I would like to take you out for tea. It's been nearly a year since we last saw each other. It would be lovely to go out again, for old time's sake. I am available in an hour. So how about it?"

"Alright! Cool. Let's go for it!"

At 55, Ryder was deep into middle age, but he still carried himself with authority. He was built like a Welsh shire carthorse, with his towering height, broad shoulders, big strong thighs, wide rump and beautiful hands. He had amazingly straight teeth and almost no body hair, except for a dash of "man hair" on his arms a wisp of hair on his chest, making him feel smooth and sleek to the touch. She'd quite forgotten how masculine and sexy he actually was.

She'd always liked his hands – from the minute he'd taken her hand in his and walked her away from Justin. They were well-groomed hands; the skin was soft, but strong and gentle at the same time. Ryder's refined, softly Australian accent was at odds with his unpretentious ways. He wasn't at all flashy. He wore suits that looked functional and comfortable and somehow made him look broader and bigger than he already was - and he always smelt really good.

Ryder was also accident prone, but all his little setbacks were like water off a duck's back. Jinny remembered a hilarious story he'd told when he had gone for an interview for a CEO position a few years back in Colombia. He had forgotten to have the last few tufts of his thinning hair cut prior to the meeting and, while shaving his beard, had thought that the quickest and easiest way to sort out the problem would be to run his razor over his head. Well, that had not worked out so well for him. In the end he had to face the board with his translator and bits of toilet paper stuck to his bleeding head and streams of sweat running down his face in the Colombian heat. Somehow he got the job even though he looked like a nursery school papier mâché project gone wrong!

Ryder was now the president of a mining company. He liked being in control, working like a precise, well-oiled machine. He was respected and liked by most of his team. Even though he was so broad and big, his accent, warm smile, steady and strong gentlemanly manners made him approachable.

Jinny got to the restaurant before he did and chose a table outside under a huge pecan tree in the garden. It was slightly secluded, a way off from the other tables, so they could do their catching up with a measure of privacy.

Jinny was nervous, yet excited to see Ryder. The more she thought about it, the more she realised that she missed their afternoon get-togethers so much! When he arrived, he looked almost exactly the same, in his old suit. But his hair was a bit greyer and he seemed a bit more world weary than he had last year.

"Hi, Jinny," he growled mischievously, kissing her on her cheek as he sat down. It was so lovely just to hear his voice. They made small talk until Ryder changed the subject…

"Jinny, it's just struck me now. You're a bit like a staffie!"

"A what?" she roared. "Now that's a first. I've never been likened to a dog before!"

"Well, when I was a little boy I used to breed Staffordshire bull terriers. The mommy would warn off anyone who came near. She was just totally focused on protecting her pups. When I put my hand under her tummy she'd growl and snarl at me for a while. Then I would gently move my hand under her belly and hold it there until she stopped growling. Then I would lift her pups out one at a time to check on them."

"Oh. So you've always been curious?"

"Well, yes. But you're like that little staffie looking after her pups. You won't let anyone get close to you. If anyone does get too close, you growl at them until you scare them off."

Jinny wasn't enjoying this conversation. She looked away and clutched at her handbag, entertaining thoughts of leaving. But Ryder took her hand.

"Now I've got your back up, haven't I, Jinny?"

"You have a little."

He gently held her hand.

"Don't go. Please stay."

She put her bag down again.

"Jinny, there is a lot about you that I don't know. And like that you're such a little staffie, I admire you for protecting and looking after your kids. That's all I was trying to say. I've missed seeing you and laughing with you. There's something about you that just makes me feel less beaten down by life. I've also got to tell you… I found our time in the hotel room quite terrifying. When you tied me up and left me there on my own… And then all of a sudden you didn't want to see me again? That was rather hurtful. And referring me to your friends for tea dates? What the hell was that all about? But I know you've had a difficult time, so I don't blame you for not trusting anyone…"

Here it was. They were going to have to discuss it all sometime.

"I'm sorry, Ryder. But you're married. I should never have done what I did."

Jinny felt ashamed of herself all over again. She didn't know what to say. She really should've just left. Ryder summoned the waiter and asked for the bill. Jinny was silent; she sat staring down at her hands in her lap. He tried again, reaching for her hand one last time.

"It's okay, Jinny. I am married and my life is complicated. And one day I'll tell you about it, but I want you to know that whatever you're going through, I will be there for you when you need me."

Then he let go of her hand. They left, and he walked her to her car.

"How about tea next week, Jinny? It's been lovely seeing you again. Same time, same place?"

"Alright. Ja. Why not!"

Why not? There were a million reasons why not! Shit, shit, shit, Jinny thought as she drove home. Why had she agreed to see Ryder again? How dumb was she? She was still young and pretty enough to have any man she wanted. Why was she agreeing to another meeting with a married man! She didn't know why she'd agreed, but she didn't really want to think about it too much either. It was palpably true that when Ryder was around she felt happy. Few men had ever cared enough to ask about her life or taken the time to understand her. When you get that again after a year of nothing, your soul laps it up like rain from heaven.

The week flew by and before Jinny knew it she and Ryder were at another restaurant chatting like they'd never been apart. They settled into a routine of breakfast and lunch meetings. So typical of a married man, though. They were always available for lunch and breakfast, seldom for dinner. That would raise the suspicions of any wife!

But she enjoyed the free lunches! She was painfully short of money.

It was shades of a story her youngest brother had once told her. When he was in London he'd been so short of cash that he had gone to donate blood just for the free cup of tea and a biscuit!

Jinny had really come to look forward to her dates with Ryder. She enjoyed getting to know him better. As he had said, his life was complicated. His kids were grown up and long out of the house. His wife had been in a terrible car accident years ago and although she had survived, her body had been mangled in the accident. The surgeons had saved her life, but the accident had caused irreparable damage to muscles, nerves and bones. She'd been left maimed and in agony. She'd spent the past few years tanking herself up on painkillers to get through every day. Ryder was a loyal husband and never expressly said that his wife was not only crippled by an accident but by an addiction too.

Ryder would never leave a wife who was unwell and Jinny respected him for that. But, as Ryder said, while everyone is busy looking after the patient, the partner dies. As duty bound as Ryder was, the reality was he was healthy, well and vibrant. He still had a wonderful life to live – in between his work commitments, his personal disappointments and whatever drama Jinny brought to the table!

Being president of a mining company had its own life of loneliness too. Everyone either bowed down to you and told you what they thought you wanted to hear, or they had an agenda. Many would try to manipulate you into getting something from you. Ryder had often said that being around Jinny made him feel younger and happier because she did neither of these things, and her only agenda was friendship.

When it came to eating out, Jinny was a creature of habit. At breakfasts it would be oats with nuts; or fruit salad with yoghurt and nuts. For lunch, chicken salad. Ryder would tease her about it. "Jinny why don't you try something different?" She would always respectfully decline and order another chicken salad. One lunch Ryder couldn't take it any longer.

"Jinny, have you ever seen a thin whale, or a thin hippo?"

"Of course not."

"Well, the only thing they eat is salads! Maybe you should try some real food."

"Do you think I'm fat?"

"Not really. I'm sure you're past your heyday a bit, but…"

Jinny could feel her eyes smarting. It was like another knife in the heart. Why did he have to say that! She forced herself to control her emotions, and managed to get through her chicken salad with chit-chat. Then she said had to rush off to a meeting. But why would Ryder say such a horrible thing! She had just started to feel more relaxed and safe around him, and now goes and hurts her. What an arse! She would not be seeing him again. Maybe she had got fat on all those lunches with him. Time to call a rain check on those and get back to gym!

Ryder called to invite her to breakfast, but she declined. He called again during the week but she passed again, saying that she was off to Cape Town for two months of school holidays. Work was slow in Jo'burg, so she was going to take advantage of the lull. Ryder accepted that and Jinny felt terribly sad. Why had he spent so much time trying to get to know her, only to hurt her again! Bloody men, she thought. The minute you start to love them they hurt you!

Jinny couldn't wait to see the kids. Luke and Skyla were growing up so fast, and she missed doing Mommy things like cooking for them, washing Skyla's hair, cutting their nails, getting their sandwiches ready for school… She loved being home with the kids. Her world felt more balanced. Ryder called her every day, asking how she was enjoying the kids. She loved their conversations, but she was still hurt by his insensitivity. She was going to gently let him down. She couldn't see him again!

Jinny couldn't bring herself to tell Ryder how she felt, so she thought that it would be best to compile an email. She spent days agonising on the best way to end their friendship. She finally sent him as pleasant an email as she could muster, saying she couldn't see him again. Ryder sent a one line response the following day. Thank you for your email Jinny, we can discuss it the next time I see you for tea. God, he was so irritating! And yet somewhere deep down she felt pleased that he was giving her space, but would not let her slip away.

Before Jinny knew it, two months were up and it was time to fly back to Jo'burg. She resumed her old position on Carol's couch and set about trying to earn a living. Skyla had already started crying five days before she left, holding and hanging onto her and pleading with Jinny to take her back to work with her.

"Mommy," Skyla had said one evening. "I love you so much and I miss you so much. I would even live in a tent in the desert with you. I don't want be away from you. Mommy, I don't care if you've got nothing left. I just want to be with you."

Jinny's heart broke, and she became more determined than ever to get back to work and get her life sorted out.

Jinny boarded her plane and cried quietly all the way back to Jo'burg. She didn't know when she was going to see the kids again and she had no idea how she was going to bring in more work. There was still no sign of the divorce being finalised, so part of her still wondered what more Justin had in store for her. All she knew for sure was that being around Ryder made her feel inordinately, irrationally happy, and he somehow made her world feel less uncertain and less out of control. On that flight to Jo'burg, Jinny had a change of heart. Perhaps more communication, not less, was the solution. She decided to see him again for another of their famous teas. Instead of cutting him off, it was time for her to tell him exactly why she was upset with him.

When Tea Day arrived, Jinny was wound like a coiled spring. She usually never confronted people with her feelings on a personal level. She was afraid of being attacked or rejected. Being married to Justin had taught her that. She felt nauseous. Having decided to confront Ryder gave her a feeling of impending doom. When he arrived he seemed upbeat and happy to see her. But he soon sensed that she was ill at ease.

"What's wrong?"

Jinny started to talk, but the words felt trapped in her throat. She felt like she was suffocating.

"Jinny," Ryder said. "Out with it! What's upsetting you?"

"Okay. Okay. The last time we met, you really upset me. You implied that I looked like a whale."

"What? When did I say you looked like a whale? I said that whales and hippos – like you – only ate green stuff and that you should try to be a bit more adventurous! Eat a variety of food."

"No, Ryder, that's not what you meant! You said I was past my heyday!"

Jinny could hear her voice rising. She wanted to leave. She pushed her chair back to get up, but Ryder reached out and grabbed her wrist.

"Jinny," he said. "Can you please just listen to me?"

Jinny started to feel hysterical. She wanted to leave now. She'd had enough. This was not going well. Speaking out about how she felt had never gone well for her. Why had she bothered to even try?

"Ryder," Jinny said, "Why would you say something so hurtful to me?"

The tears came. Ryder put his face against her face and held her wrists in her lap.

"Shhh, shhh, Jinny. There, there. It's not so bad."

Right there, something in Jinny snapped. She started to scream.

"Don't touch me! Let me go!"

She wrenched her hands free from Ryder and leapt from her seat. She grabbed her bag and ran to the car. She needed to get away, she needed to hide. Her world was not safe, she needed to get away. She jumped into the car and sped off.

Oh my God. She knew she should not have tried to confront Ryder. She should have just said no thanks to seeing him again and avoided the conversation entirely. Speaking out about how she felt never went well!

She had been tense from the outset, but the conversation had gone south as soon as Ryder had held her wrists and told her to shhhhh. It was the shhhhh that had really set her off.

After that, Jinny ignored Ryder's calls. She didn't trust herself with him at the moment. She felt like screaming and attacking him simultaneously. For now she would just trust her gut feeling to stay away from him entirely.

Jinny felt helpless, useless and powerless again, a "suitcase" case who slept on a friend's couch and couldn't seem to get anything together. She wished that she was brave enough to take out a butcher's knife and run full speed at a wall and thrust it through her useless, palpitating heart. She was so tired of feeling like she was on a mortician's table, tired of feeling that her happiness and wellbeing were controlled by other people. That feeling had to stop. Anything was better than this.

***

THEN, LIKE A glimmer of light in the darkness, Christiaan called and invited her to tea at his office again. She had been avoiding him for months. She had really enjoyed his touch and she wanted more. So what if he was a bit of a slut. Right now, everything about Jinny felt numb and feeling anything would be better than feeling nothing.

They met for tea and it was pleasant enough. Christiaan teased her and joked with her like they had done when they were younger. It felt good to be with such a gentle, loving soul. Afterwards, he walked her out. At the car, he kissed her gently, then wrapped his arms around her and slid his hands down her back onto her bum. He pulled her into his body and it felt like the sun coming out.

"Jinny," he said. "I really want you."

"I really want you too. Why don't you follow me to my friend's place? She is out at the moment. We can play there."

Jinny didn't care any longer. She just wanted to feel something other than helpless, hopeless and useless. Chris found her sexy and desirable, and she so desperately wanted to feel loved for just a little while. He got into the passenger seat.

"Okay, Jinny. Let's go. When you're ready.

She started the car and headed home.

"Jinny," Chris said, "You need to focus on the road and I am going to focus on you. I am going to pleasure and please you and take my time with you. This isn't about me, Jinny. This is all about you. You're in control and I am here entirely to pleasure you."

A thrill ran up her spine. Christiaan didn't want to dominate or control or hurt her. He just wanted to please her and that really turned her on. She could feel her crotch getting hot and her panties getting wet. OMG. Chris was good at this. He hadn't even touched her yet and she was lubricating and wanting more already.

Jinny focused on the road and Chris slid his hand under her shirt, lifted her bra and began fondling her nipples. His touch was light and tantalising. She wished he'd touch her harder but he kept teasing. He leaned in and kissed her cheek, her ear.

"Jinny, can I slide my hand into your pants?"

No one had ever asked her permission before.

"Yes."

He slid his hand in. She was slippery and he expertly slipped his index finger between her lips and started to move rhythmically, slowly up and down, easing his finger into the opening. OMG. She liked what he was doing. Her jeans were tight, so she spread her legs wider to give him more access. But the front of her jeans were still zipped and as she opened her legs, it pulled them tighter on her body, pushing Chris's finger deep inside her. Fuck, that finger felt good.

"Jinny," he said. "Jinny. You're so sexy. So wet. Do you want me to carry on?"

"Yes. Yes!"

He squeezed his finger deeper into her. He pulled up her top and gently sucked on her nipple. Fortunately, the traffic was quiet, but by now she didn't care who might be watching. She just wanted more. They were nearly home.

"Chris," she said. I need you to stop."

"Your wish is my command."

He stopped sucking on her nipple, but kept his hand inside her. He squeezed her vulva gently with the rest of his hand. Oh, my freaking God. Even that felt good. She parked in the garage. Christiaan removed his hand and stepped out of the car towards the interleading door. Jinny walked to open the door, but Chris swung her around and pushed her gently up against the door. He kissed her with tongue. Jeezes, she wanted that tongue.

"Jinny?"

"Yes?"

"Tell me what you want me to do to you."

"I want you to kiss my other lips."

She grabbed him by the shoulders and pushed him to his knees.

He unzipped her pants and pulled them down. He slid her panties to the side, took her swollen lips in his mouth and sucked them voraciously. God, that felt good, Her legs began to quiver. She arched her back, spreading her legs wider. She needed him to thrust those fingers into her again. She was groaning now. She couldn't help herself.

Christiaan stood and opened the door. He swept her up and walked into the lounge, where he put her down on the couch. He removed her pants, then he was on his knees again, tasting her, licking her.

"Mmmmm, Jinny," he gasped. "You taste so good. I just want to drink you and drown in your wetness."

His words were such a mad turn-on. No one had ever said that to her before. She opened her legs wider and he moved forward, sucking her lips while flicking his tongue over her clit. Her legs quivered and she could no longer control her gasping moans. She didn't care, it just felt so, so good. Now he slid two fingers in, slowly at first, then he picked up speed. He was massaging her G-spot, Oh God, how much more of this pleasure she could take before she started coming!

"Chris, you've got me close to coming."

He looked up with a face covered in her liquid.

"Do you want me to penetrate you, Jinny, or do you want to come with me licking you?"

No one had ever asked her that. The control thrilled her even more

"I want you to fuck me from behind."

He stood and picked her up, positioning her over the arm of the couch. He ran his hands over her bottom, up her back and then back down to her legs. He spread them apart, then eased his fingers rhythmically into her again. Oh, yes. She just wanted him to fuck her now.

"Chris? Please enter me now."

"Ask me again."

"Chris! I want you to fuck me now!"

He parted her butt cheeks, ran his finger lightly around her perineum and then pushed his finger just inside her anus, while simultaneously penetrating her pussy with his dick. He moved his dick and his finger rhythmically in and out of her. She wanted to open herself even wider to him. She wanted him to fuck her now.

"Fuck me," she said. "I want you to fuck me harder."

He withdrew his finger, then gripped her hips and thrust himself deeper into her.

"I want you to fuck me, Chris. I want you to pound me so hard that my tits shake." He pulled her onto him and took her with animal urgency now. She could feel herself losing all control. She was coming now. As she started to come, her vaginal muscles pulsing, she felt Chris climaxing. He cried out as his load gushed out inside her. She felt his body jerking and twitching. It all just felt so good.

They slumped over on the couch, spent. He pulled out of her and removed the condom he had used. He knotted the condom and pushed it down the side of the couch. She made a mental note to flush it later.

"God," she said. "That felt good!"

"Ja," he laughed. "You're quite a hot lover."

"Well, best you call an Uber to get you back to work."

With that she jumped over the couch, grabbed her pants and flung him his undies and trousers. His taxi arrived within seven minutes and she was just about able to walk him to the door on unsteady legs.

"Chris, you're such a slut."

They both laughed at that, and he was gone.

OMG. She felt well and truly shagged. Oh well, she smiled to herself, at least this time it was in a good way. Even if it was only for a few moments, Jinny felt loved, special and connected. Who cares that Christiaan was married, so was she! And just once didn't really count, did it? She didn't love Chris and he didn't love her. It was just sex.

***

THE COMPLEXITIES OF real life returned the next day. Ryder called.

"Jinny," he said. "I really don't know what has upset you so much, but I apologise. Perhaps you interpreted our conversation the wrong way. But I'm sorry for upsetting you so. Please can we meet for coffee?"

Jinny agreed. And this time she didn't berate herself for agreeing to go out with a married man. She just missed Ryder. She felt more stable when he was in her life. He certainly cared about her. Christiaan didn't care about her, he was just someone familiar.

She felt excited about seeing Ryder again, but anxious at the same time. She didn't want to have another meltdown, and she wasn't entirely sure what that last meltdown had been all about.

Ryder met her in his work canteen. He was wearing one of his old suits, with mismatched shirt and tie again. Something about him not being absolutely perfect always made Jinny smile. That deep, husky voice, those brown eyes with their speckles of green… his strong long legs and his hands... Ryder really had beautiful hands.

As Jinny scanned the menu, a familiar tight feeling came over her – she just really wanted the chicken salad. Hopefully Ryder wouldn't mention the whale thing again! She would wait until he'd placed his order and then place her own. The waiter returned.

"I'll have one beef burger with chips please," said Ryder. "And one chicken salad."

He smiled at her.

"It's okay, Jinny. For the past three years you've always ordered the same thing for lunch and I don't think that's going to change."

He patted her on the hand as the waiter took the menus away. Jinny could feel herself start to relax a bit. The meal and company were pleasant. Ryder had not been a marketing director for nothing. He had excellent conversation skills and knew how to veer away from difficult topics when he needed to. They seldom ate pudding after their meals, but today Jinny really felt like ice-cream and hot chocolate sauce. Ryder ordered the cheesecake. They chatted like old times again and Jinny lapped up the cosy, reassuring warmth of Ryder's laughter. He had a laugh that bubbled out from the depths of him like a warm spring. She loved that laugh.

After the meal, Ryder walked her through the gardens of his office park back to her car.

"Jinny," he said. "I don't wish to upset you in any way but I do want to understand what happened the last time we met. I gripped your wrists because I was trying to calm you down. I could see you were working yourself up into a state. But you… you didn't calm down! You looked like a terrified child! What was it? You got even more terrified… almost aggressive. Then you charged off…"

My God. Why did he have to bring this up? When they had just had such a lovely lunch! She started to back away from him. She was nearly at her car now. She just wanted to get out of there before there was another scene.

But it seemed he wouldn't let her leave.

"Jinny, please don't go. I am trying to understand what happened."

"Ryder," she said, "I am not entirely sure what happened the last time, but you're right. When you gripped my arms and told me to 'Shhhhhh…' I felt absolutely terrified and trapped. I needed to leave…"

Now she had that same feeling again.

"Why does 'Shhh' upset you so much?"

As he said it, Jinny remembered being held down and violated as a child. The fear, the utter, utter powerlessness...

"Jinny?" he asked. "What is going on? Why are you crying?"

She couldn't speak now. The tears were pouring down her cheeks. He held her and she just sobbed her pain into his chest. He held her tight and stroked her hair, waiting until the sobbing had subsided. Then he asked again: "Jinny, why are you crying? Why does that upset you so much?"

She pulled back.

"Because I was repeatedly raped when I was a child! Okay? Is that want you want to hear? Do you really want to know why?

She felt the hysteria bubbling just below the surface. But she was keeping it at bay. He'd asked. He said he wanted to know. Well, now he would get the whole story.

"This man used to hold me down by my wrists and say, 'Shhhhh, shhhh, shhhh…' While he was attacking me!"

She started to sob again.

"Good God, Jinny!"

Again he wrapped her in his arms and held her tight. The pain was all coming out now, in a series of sobbing convulsions. He waited until she'd recovered somewhat, then he gently held her at arm's length and looked her in the eyes.

"Jinny, I am so incredibly sorry that that happened to you. You really did not deserve that. No one deserves that. You are such an amazing girl."

No one had ever said they were sorry about those attacks. No one had ever said she was amazing.

When her mom had found out, she had called her a "very bad girl", and accused her of trying to steal her husband away from her. She was told to keep quiet, told not to tell anyone about it. Something like that would tarnish their family name. So Jinny was shipped off to a private girls' boarding school. That was her mom's way of ensuring that "she didn't get herself into any more trouble."

Once Jinny had stopped crying, Ryder walked her to her car and opened the door for her. He gave her a kiss on the cheek and promised he'd never use that word with her or hold her wrists like that again.

She drove home sobbing like a baby. By the time she got back she was exhausted. She collapsed on the couch and fell asleep.

Ryder called the next day to ask how she was. Mercifully, he didn't mention the conversation. Jinny had not consciously thought about what had happened to her when she was a child. Since she'd left that behind, she didn't want to think about it at all!

✳✳✳

HE CLEARLY FELT that she needed a bit of a break, because he booked them both a day at a health spa on a game farm. He was even taking a day off work. It was actually a great idea. A day away with Ryder would be lovely.

They met at the health hydro, where he'd booked two full body massages, a flotation tank session and some Jacuzzi time.

Once she'd changed into her robe, Jinny stood waiting for Ryder with their two masseuses. He was in the changing room for ages! Jinny decided to knock.

"Ryder, are you okay in there? What's taking so long?"

"To be honest, I've never been to a health hydro before. I don't know what to keep on and what to take off."

"Ryder, you Wally," she laughed. "Just keep your undies on. Put on the robe and the slippers and come through. The massage people are waiting for us."

Wow. He'd never even been to a health hydro before. But he'd gone to the effort of booking an entire day for them. So sweet.

She giggled as Ryder emerged from the bathroom in his robe and slippers. He looked a bit like Hugh Hefner – just a younger, sexier version.

Jinny had assumed that the therapists would take them into separate rooms for their massages, but it seemed they were to share a room. She gently enquired from them whether this was standard. Here Ryder piped up.

"Jinny, I have never had anyone massage my body before, apart from you that one day. I feel quite nervous, so I thought it would be nice for us to be in the same room.

Again she gave him the benefit of the doubt. His shyness was cute.

She stood by Ryder's massage bed as he grappled with the logistics of the massage.

"Why is there a hole in the bed? Is that for my willy?"

She couldn't help laughing at that.

"No Ryder, that's for your face, you idiot!"

With that, she hopped onto her massage table to show him how it was done.

He, in turn, hopped onto his bed and the massage therapists stepped forward to get to work. They unobtrusively removed their gowns, placing towels over their waists and legs.

Jinny closed her eyes and let her female massage therapist work her magic on the knots in her back. Halfway through her back massage, Ryder had still not been able to surrender to the moment.

"Would you mind if I held your hand?"

At this, the therapists pushed their massage tables together so that Ryder and Jinny could lie hand in hand. His handsome hands felt as good as they looked, and she felt warm and safe in his reassuring grasp as her therapist went to work.

When they wobbled in a blissful wooze from the massage rooms, it was time for the flotation tank. This was a shallow, circular tank filled with warm salt water. The idea is that you float in a bubble of sensory deprivation, the water your exact body temperature, in the dark, as underwater speakers play classical music. Well, from the minute Jinny got into the tank her legs began to burn from the salt. After a minute, her fanny started to burn too. Then she got some salt water in her eye. She couldn't remember where she'd put her towel, so she was groping around in the dark when she bumped into Ryder. By this stage his eyes were also burning and he was also searching for his towel.

"Now I know why this tank de-stresses you," he said. "You just feel grateful to be alive when you get out of it!"

They chuckled through the salty tears, as they crawled blindly around the tank..

"Ouch!" he gasped. "I've just scraped my knee. It's burning, but I can't see if it's bleeding because it's so bloody dark! How long have we been in here. When do you think they'll come for us?"

They collapsed into more laughter, and then Ryder finally found his towel. He positioned it behind his neck on the side of the tank and pulled her towards him by the foot. She crawled up next to him, and thus positioned, they sat hand-in-hand in the dark, giggling like kids. Bodies itching like they were on fire the whole time!

As soon as the door opened, they both rushed for the showers to rinse the salt water from their burning skin. Then it was time for the next adventure – a nice, big, warm Jacuzzi session!

Ryder had organised champers and grapes, and they lounged in the Jacuzzi eating grapes, sipping champers and chatting. She didn't drink as a rule, but the combination of the divine massage, a jolly good giggle and the bliss of bobbing around in the bubbles holding Ryder's hand made it feel right. She rested her head on the edge of the Jacuzzi, closed her eyes and let the bubbles lift her body to the surface. She felt Ryder move in close. He snuggled in and kissed her on the lips. She was so relaxed and happy and the kiss felt good. She kissed him back.

This sparked a new urgency in him. He straddled her, cradling her head in his hands and kissing her again. She melted into him as she ran her hands down his back and over his bottom. She reached down and grabbed his massive dick. Wow.

"Hold me, Jinny."

She gripped his dick harder and he moaned, then seemed to give in to his animal lust. He splashed on top of her, preparing to take her completely. Then there was a polite knock on the door.

"Time's up!"

Just as well. Things were about to get out of hand! They dressed, then wandered over to the restaurant for lunch. She just felt happy. She wasn't going to worry about tomorrow or the day after, she was just going to focus on enjoying the time that she had with Ryder today.

Lunch was lovely. But it took a serious turn when Ryder told her about his mom being attacked on their farm when he was about ten. He had watched his mom being assaulted and had somehow managed to get the three assailants to stop attacking her. After the incident, she had suffered post-traumatic stress and depression. His parents then sent him to boarding school. There he had sorely missed home and his parents and endured daily jacks and hidings from a sadistic housemaster. She realised Ryder was really a caring man who hated injustice and bullying, because he had experienced injustice as a child.

"Enough about me, Jinny," he said, seeming to snap out of his nostalgic reverie. "I've booked the bridal suite for us to go and relax in until dinner tonight."

He signed for lunch and ordered a double whisky and a Coke Lite for her. Then they ambled along to the suite. It had the most divine balcony and a view of the dam, where buck, zebra and elephants came to drink. They lounged on the patio, at perfect ease with each other. They propped their feet up on the table, sipped their drinks and enjoyed the silence.

Jinny had no change of clothing – she hadn't realised they would be staying for the night. But she really wanted to shower before supper. What a treat! Sleeping in a bed tonight instead of on Carol's couch! Ryder wanted to look around a bit, which gave her a perfect opportunity to shower, wash her hair and get ready for supper.

She showered, then wrapped herself in a towel and came through to the bedroom to retrieve her clothes. There she was a bit surprised to find Ryder. He had come back and was lying naked on the bed. He had lovely lush, but greying, chest hair.

"Jinny," he said. "Come here."

She walked over to the bed and dropped her towel. Ryder pulled her onto him; she plunged her hands into his chest hair, then slid them up onto his face. She turned his head to the side and stuck her tongue into his ear. He moaned and arched his body, pulling her closer. He claimed her mouth with his, then whipped her onto her back and pinned her down with his leg. She gasped and tried to wiggle away. Ryder looked at her with no emotion, just lust. He released her legs, then leapt up, pulling her onto the floor with him. He sat with his back against the couch.

"Sit on me."

She did as she was told. He was not erect yet but OMG, she wanted that big dick inside her. She devoured him with a kiss, running her hands over his chest and squeezing his nipples.

"Jinny," he gasped. "Jinny. Squeeze them harder."

She took his nipple in her mouth and nibbled. He flinched, but she only sucked him harder. Then she slid off his crotch, down between his legs and took his half-erect dick in her mouth. She held the base of his cock and sucked him deep into her throat. Ryder let out a moan and gripped her hair, holding her head down on his cock.

"Ohhh, Jinny!"

He was hard and erect now. She stood.

"Jinny. Come, sit on me."

Again did as she was told, straddling him and easing his big, hard cock into her. He was so big. Even though she was wet it was a tight fit. But so good! Really, really, good. She rocked her hips on him, grinding and stimulating her clit with the friction of his penis moving in and out of her.

"Touch yourself."

She arched her back and circled her breasts. Ryder moved his hand to her clit and began rubbing her. He wasn't doing it right. She pushed his hand away and stimulated herself in the way she knew - the way that pleased her.

He watched her, mesmerised. Then he grabbed her hips and began moving her harder and faster on his dick, grinding her hips into his.

"Are you nearly there, Jinny? I want you to come first."

"Mmmmm."

"Come, Jinny! Come! I don't know how much longer I can hold out!"

So damn sexy! She moved faster, but she wanted him to come first. She wanted him to lose control. She ground her hips into his, falling forward and kissing him long and hungry until he was almost gasping for air.

"Jinny! I can't hold on much longer! Come with me, Jinny! Come with me!"

She could feel her body reaching orgasm. Spasms tore through her as she felt him exploding inside her.

She slumped onto him gasping for breath. He clung to her as the last warm shudders of orgasm shook their bodies. Then he rolled onto his side, spooning her on the floor.

"Jinny?"

"Yes, Ryder?"

"That was so good."

They giggled like kids, still warm and cosy, as the fire of lust gently simmered down.

"You're worth more than this," he said.

She didn't know what he meant by that, but she didn't want to analyse it right now. Instead she wiggled her hips into his groin, held his arms wrapped around her and drifted off to sleep.

She awoke the next morning in bed, with Ryder still beside her. He must have carried her to bed during the night. They had to rush because Ryder needed to be at work. They showered and dressed, then dashed to the buffet area for breakfast. As Ryder was gulping down a coffee, and out of nowhere, he blurted out, "You would marry me if I asked, wouldn't you?" Then he smiled a curious smile…

WTF? How dare he ask something like that! He was still married to someone else! What was he thinking? She looked him squarely in the eye.

"No, Ryder. I wouldn't marry you."

She barely held herself back from continuing, "…because you're a lying, cheating, bastard, just like the rest of them!"

God, sometimes he made her blood boil! He could make her so angry so quickly.

They could be ambling along, having the most amazing time and then he would just destroy the moment, shatter that ambience by saying something completely out of line! He seemed to have a knack for this. It reminded her of the time they'd met a woman who told them she was a general practitioner. Ryder couldn't help blurting out to her as they left, "Nice meeting you, Doc. I hope I never have to see you again!"

He'd seemed quite pleased with his little joke, oblivious to how insensitive and offensive it might have been.

Jinny didn't want to seem ungracious, so she excused herself from the table, saying she really needed to get to work. She gave Ryder a peck on the cheek and left.

Wow. What a crazy, unexpected and wonderful adventure! She'd really enjoyed her day and night with Ryder. Now she assumed he'd start feeling guilty about it and wouldn't contact her for weeks. Until he felt his urge for sex overwhelm him again – then things would miraculously thaw and he'd get back in touch again.

As Jinny had anticipated, Ryder did not contact her the next day. She felt a bit sad about being right. Why did she so desperately want Ryder to be different from all the other guys she had ever met? And what were the chances of that anyway? Why couldn't she just accept that she was nothing more than a plaything to him? Why was she doing this, and why did she keep going back to him!

***

AT ANY RATE, she was counselling the whole day to help her patients manage their crises, so she had little time to think about her own dramas. Her latest patient really topped the charts on the dysfunction level. In fact, she had never had a client as funny and as dysfunctional as he was.

He was a prim, well-spoken Englishman, short in stature. He wore cream, cotton Parisian suits with matching ties and handkerchiefs, always with a handkerchief in the top pocket. Though the hankie was purely an accessory. Jinny could only imagine the horror on his face if some damsel in distress ever asked to blow her nose on his precious hankie! He drove a cream Rolls-Royce and she often wondered if he'd had the seat customised so he could see over the steering wheel. He always smelt of Kent soap, a traditional Englishman's soap with a whiff of surgical chemicals. He fancied himself a creature of superior intelligence. Considering he was one of the best reconstructive plastic surgeons in SA, he had some justification for such hubris. He came across as a stately gentleman. He'd introduced himself to Jinny in a demure tone, saying, "Good morning, Ms Gent. I am Mr Bushmore." Jinny thought she'd perhaps heard wrong. But upon looking at his patient file, she realised that, yes, his surname was in fact Bushmore!

Good God, what an unfortunate name! She decided to give him a secret nickname to avoid bursting out laughing every time she thought about his surname. So he became the Duke.

The Duke not only had the most gifted hands for surgery but also an eye for beautiful things. It was this that had led him astray and into a few too many "bushes". He really needed to bush less and not more!

His penchant for beautiful women had surfaced long before his wife's affair and her confession that the cum of her personal trainer tasted better than his. With him being a small man, with a small dick, enormous ego and a bigger bank balance, this boded ill for their relationship. Frankly, it had sent the little Duke right over the edge. It not only saw him downing litres of pineapple juice to improve the taste of his cum, but also created an all-consuming desire to shove his dick down the throats of as many women as possible to reaffirm himself. His clients were generally insecure, beautiful women, and he had the skill and ability to make those women even more beautiful. So these women tended to elevate him to demigod status. There were ample opportunities to take advantage of his elevated position, and he had no compunction in doing that.

A call girl visited his offices at least once a week, and there were three patients in different areas of Jo'burg who needed regular "post-op check-ups". Then there was one patient he was madly in love with… and a wife. This was over and above his weekly consultations and surgeries. He was burning the candle at both ends. He "managed" the stress of it all by drinking copious amounts of alcohol and taking a pre-med called Dormicum at night. It was only a matter of time before he took one Dormi too many, or one more whisky before bed that saw him never waking up.

One side-effect of the Dormicum-alcohol combination was wiping out huge chunks of his short-term memory and his conscience. It also made him more reckless and uninhibited sexually.

The Duke was a prime example of how dysfunctional a ridiculously successful person could be. And as dysfunctional and insane as his antics were, he was incredibly funny. It was up to Jinny to counsel him and to get him to a point where he could acknowledge he had a problem. If she could just get him to slow down on the Dormicum and whisky he might slow down on the women and the wild extracurricular behaviour too. That might get him to a point where he could decide whether he really wanted to stay with a woman who had swallowed her personal trainer's cum on the table in their cellar. Or whether he was able to forgive her and move on. It never crossed the Duke's mind that his behaviour was far worse than anything his wife had ever done – in his mind he had just had a few indiscretions.

Jinny was sure that if his wife knew what he was really up to, she would probably shoot him on the spot. But, all in all, they sounded like the kind of dysfunctional pair that would stay together forever, firmly locked in their own game of pain and betrayal.

The Duke made her own little dalliances seem quite tame by comparison.

At the Duke's previous consultation he had been obsessing about his genital and anal hair and what he should do to get rid of it. Jinny had patiently gone through the options with him: laser hair removal, waxing, Veeting… Then, this week he had given her a blow-by-blow debrief on his genital hair removal exploits. It was so hilarious that he had her literally rolling on the floor with laughter.

It has started with the Duke deciding to Veet. Although he had read the fine print warning against using the product near the genital area, he had chosen to go ahead anyway. This was a bad idea. The process culminated in him lying spread-eagled in bed with his balls and anus covered in Veet, his knees behind his ears. He had to pull his butt cheeks apart while he put his overhead ceiling fan on at full speed to try to soothe the chemical burn on his anus. Apparently it felt like it was literally on fire. His story destroyed every last shred of professional reserve she had. Jinny collapsed into a giggling fit. She simply couldn't help herself. That image of him lying on his bed in the roast-chicken position, arse in the breeze… it was all just too vivid.

"Jinny?" the Duke asked. "Are you laughing at me?"

"Absolutely," she replied. "Your story is funnier than any woman's Brazilian wax story I've heard!"

"Well, that was only the start of it. To add insult to injury I only realised upon removing my anal hair that it was impossible to fart quietly. One day in surgery, I landed up doing a cheek-wobbling, earth-shattering fart. It startled the hell out of my nurses, and had everyone chuckling underneath their surgical masks."

Jinny roared with laughter all over again.

"In summary, Jinny, I've decided that anal hair removal is not for me."

The Duke was dysfunctional - there was no getting away from it. He may even be beyond redemption, but Jinny liked to think that anyone could be saved if they chose to be. Needless to say, despite his dysfunctional, deviant behaviour, he was hilarious. Jinny enjoyed having him as a patient, because in a way he made her feel better about her own level of dysfunction. And he made her laugh. If Jinny could just convince him to slow down on the drinking and the Dormicum, he might actually have a chance of pulling his life together.

***

"CHRISTIAAN? JINNY HERE".

"Hi, Jinny. Have you been missing me?"

"Chris, you know I never miss you when we're apart. I'm not calling to talk about work or the kids, I'm calling for one reason only. I think you know what it is. Are you available for some sundowner sex tonight?"

"Of course I am, Jinny. You know I'm always up for that with you."

Just the prospect of some imminent loving, made Jinny feel calmer and more in control again. Though she'd never tell Christiaan, it was a feeling of being out of control that had driven her to make the call. As she'd hoped, she was now chilling out nicely. She went home to tidy up and get herself ready. Luckily for her, Carol was away on a contract and she had the entire place to herself.

Christiaan arrived around 5pm. They probably had an hour and a half for sex. But the time limit meant there was no need for chit-chat. It was going to be sex, nothing more.

Christiaan stepped in through the front door and she closed it behind him. He pushed her up against it and kissed her gently on the lips.

"God, Jinny. You are such a hot woman. What do you want me to do to you today? Your wish is my command."

That kind of talk really made her feel better.

"I want you to get down on your knees in front of me. I want you to pull my panties down and I want you to suck my clit and lick my labia until I can hardly stand."

She never felt shy around Chris. She didn't worry if her bum was too fat, or if her legs were wobbly, or if she was good enough for him. She didn't love him anyway, so she wasn't worried about whether she pleased him or not. She could just focus on how she wanted him to please her.

"Oh, Jinny, you're so hot. You know I really want to pleasure you."

He nibbled on her lower lip as he unbuttoned her top and expertly unhooked her bra. He slid his hands up onto her breasts and squeezed them, gently rolling her nipples between his thumb and forefingers. Jinny could feel herself lubricating. OMG, she loved that gentle touch. It thrilled her, made her long for more.

Christiaan bent down and took one of her nips in his mouth, sucking it as he flicked his tongue over the tip, simultaneously rolling the other nipple between his fingers. He was in no rush, he sucked harder on her nipple and she felt her body warm to his touch. He swopped nipples – sucking and caressing in the opposite formation. Her body arched towards him, demanding more. He moved up and kissed her on the mouth again as his hand explored the front of her pants, His fingers were between her lips, inside her vadge. Jinny gasped. He gripped her vulva, moving down and kissing her nipple again.

He withdrew his fingers and knelt in front of her as instructed. He pulled down her panties and her skirt, leaving them lying around her ankles. He brought his fingers up to his nose and sniffed them like a hound on a scent. He licked them clean.

"Mmm. Your smell. You taste so good. I want to drown myself in your juices!" She felt his lust. This wasn't just acceptance. He wanted her desperately! She grabbed

Christiaan's head and pulled it into her crotch.

"Suck me! Lick me now!"

He pressed her up against the wall, spreading her legs wide as he smothered his lips across her wetness. He slavered on her lips, flicking his tongue across her clit while easing two fingers deep inside her.

The pleasure was almost unbearable. Her body shuddered. She just wanted to tear her legs wide open, to let him right inside her. She could feel her lubrication flowing out of her body and the sound of Chris lapping it up and swallowing it. It thrilled her to her very core.

Christiaan stood, raised her up and carried her bodily to the bedroom, gasping with the urgency of it all. He lowered her gently onto the bed with her legs hanging over the edge. She flopped backwards, surrendering to the moment. Let him do what he wanted. He spread her legs, again plunging his fingers in and out of her, with his tongue also desperately darting inside her. He was jabbing his tongue as deep as it would go, flickering it stiffly inside her. God, she really, really liked that.

"Christiaan, you're going to make me come this way. Is this what you want?"

"This is not about what I want, it's about what you want. What do you want?"

"I want you to get up and put a condom on your dick and I want you to slide it inside of me."

Christiaan did as he was told.

He had a long, thin dick – nothing to write home about. But his tongue and fore-play technique were out of this world.

He thrust in and out of her a few times until she stopped him.

"What would you like me to do to you, Jinny?"

"I want you to make me cum with your tongue and your fingers only."

He willingly obliged and within seconds Jinny felt her body climaxing, electric pulses of pure pleasure coursing through her

"Oh, God! Oh, God! Oh, God! Yes, yes, yes!

Soon she was laughing as the dopamine rush of pleasure consumed her.

"Oh God, Chris. That was really good."

Once the first rush of pleasure had subsided into the warm, sunset afterglow, she sat up, and went to fetch her panties and skirt.

"Thanks, Chris," she told him when she returned. "You have exactly three minutes to gather your things."

And she waved towards the door, in case there was any doubt. He knew the score, though.

"Jinny, that was really good… I'll see you some time when you're horny again."

"You're still such a slut," she laughed as she shut the door.

There would be no chit-chat, no emails, no SMS correspondence, and Jinny liked that. There was something quite honest about not pretending to be more than what they were. They were just friends getting together and shagging each other's brains out every now and then. This wasn't love, it was purely and simply sex on Jinny's terms. She liked that.

When she was really cross with Ryder, shagging Chris made her feel better. She wasn't sure why, but who cares? They were all a bunch of cheats and Ryder hated giving her oral sex anyway. Why should she feel bad? She wasn't going to spend too much time thinking about it. It was just sex.

***

IT WAS 8PM when Ryder called.

"Jinny? I just called to say thank you for such a special time. I really enjoyed myself and I really enjoyed you."

Wow, she thought. This was a first – the first time anyone had ever thanked her for sex.

She felt ecstatic that he'd called. Maybe he was a bit different after all. As if reading her mind, he gallantly invited her to breakfast the next day and she accepted.

There had been a subtle change in Ryder's behaviour. These days there was something kinder and softer about him when he spoke to her.

"Jinny, don't you think it's funny how we can rip our clothes off and shag each other one day and then a few days later be sitting at a table fully clothed having a cordial conversation again?"

"Yes, Ryder. It is odd, although I must say I did rather enjoy your state of undress," And they both erupted into laughter.

"Well, I enjoyed your state of undress too… Jinny, you would say yes if I asked you to marry me wouldn't you?"

She was completely taken aback. How could he ask such an insensitive question knowing full well that she was going through a terrible divorce herself? How presumptuous and arrogant of him! What made him think she would ever entertain the idea of marrying a cheat?

"No! Ryder, the answer would be no! I could never marry you."

With that, she burst into tears, grabbed her handbag and left.

"Thank you for breakfast," she sobbed over her shoulder as she made for the door. He would certainly be paying for her again, the bastard.

In how many ways did she despise Ryder at this moment? Why did he always have to ruin things with his insensitive, stupid questions? For a company president, he was incredibly clumsy, just so tactless in his choice of words.

How did he always manage to infuriate her so? Without fail!

Predictably, Ryder called the next day to find out how she was.

"Are you suffering from PMS?"

WTF! That made her even madder. What made a man think that any time a woman took exception to something, she must have PMS? And if not that, then she must be unstable or insane!

"No, Ryder! I don't have PMS. But I can tell you that I really hate you!"

"Okay… That's a good starting point. Let's have lunch tomorrow and you can tell me why you hate me. I don't understand why you got so upset. I wanted to know if you'd say yes if I asked you to marry me."

"Now I really, really hate you, Ryder!"

"That's okay. Let's discuss it tomorrow."

"Fine!"

Jinny was tense again. She really didn't want to get into a state like the last time she'd tried to explain to Ryder what he'd done wrong.

Ryder was already at the lunch table when she arrived. His face looked taut and drawn, his lips were thin and his eyes were stormy but without malice. They ordered lunch and Ryder was careful not to touch her. He'd clearly learnt from experience that it was unwise to touch her when she was upset.

"Jinny, do you want to tell me why you were so upset about what I said the other day?"

She could feel that trapdoor closing on her mouth again, could feel the fear rising in her throat. It was that same old feeling that made her want to pick up her handbag and run out of the door. Her heart began pounding in her chest. No, she couldn't tell him. She instinctively grabbed for her bag and stood up to leave. This time Ryder didn't try to grab her or even stand up. He stayed seated exactly where he was and said in a steady, calm voice, "Jinny, please stay, so we can sort this out. I'm not going to shout at you, and I don't want to hurt you in any way. I just want to understand what I've done to upset you so."

Jinny stared at Ryder. Now she really hated him even more. To come with the whole decent, caring spiel. She stood there staring at him. She opened her mouth to talk but her voice felt trapped in her throat.

"Jinny, it's okay. Take your time," he said. "I understand it's difficult for you to speak about things that upset you, but I'll wait for you."

Finally she was able to say quietly, almost inaudibly, "Because you're married, Ryder. Don't you think it's presumptuous to ask me if I'd marry you when you are married?"

Her voice developed a momentum. She felt her confidence growing as she warmed to her theme.

"You're not just a little married. You're very married, and in no position to ask such a question."

The tears rolled down Jinny's cheeks again.

"Thank you," he said. "Thank you for being honest with me. Now sit down and have some tea so we can talk about it."

She felt vulnerable for having cried, but he really seemed to want to make it right. "May I please say something," he said as she sipped her tea. She nodded.

"Jinny, I apologise for upsetting you. I didn't realise how insensitive that was. It's just… I think that you deserve more than what we're doing. You're a good person. You don't deserve what has happened to you; you deserve to be happily married and I suppose in my own clumsy way that is what I was trying to say."

No one had ever apologised to Jinny for upsetting her. So she appreciated Ryder's apology and she felt a bit bad about the fuck-you sex with Chris. But should she feel bad? After all, Ryder still had a wife to snuggle up to at night.

***

THE DYSFUNCTIONAL DUKE had booked an appointment and Jinny was looking forward to seeing him. She hoped he'd taken her advice and slowed down on the Dormicum and whisky. Much to her surprise, he had.

In their last session, Jinny had asked him to write up a pros-and-cons list of everyone that he was involved with. The idea was that he would consider what the consequences of his actions would be if he was caught out.

For today's session, she was going to get him to talk her through his list.

At the top of his list was his wife.

"Wife: Pros – He loved her; she was the most beautiful women he had ever met; she was the mother of his children, and although he did not like the way she belittled and humiliated him, he felt that he deserved it.

Cons – He could not get over her affair with the personal trainer and her swallowing his cum. But more than that, the trainer had been taller than him, with a bigger dick. That actually upset him the most.

She didn't like oral sex – giving or receiving – and he really wanted someone to suck his cock until he came. He had been at an all-boy's private school in Natal. Three of them used to get together regularly and suck each other's cocks until they came. This was where he'd really developed a taste for cock sucking.

Call girl: Pros: He'd found her in an escort ad in the newspaper a few years ago. At that time his wife had had their child and didn't want to have sex with him. She was just tired all the time. He'd gone through a few escorts, but had finally settled on one who came to his practice after hours every week.

She would allow him to suck her pussy. He could shove his dick as far down her throat as he wanted to, without her gagging. And she would swallow his cum. He regularly tested himself and her for HIV, STDs and STIs, and so far they were both clear. So his patients didn't have to worry about contracting HIV from him during surgery.

Cons: He suspected that he'd get into a bit of trouble if anyone found out about her. It was frowned upon by society. But he paid her handsomely to keep her mouth shut and he didn't need to worry about her falling in love with him. She was a prostitute after all.

Patients: Pros: All three of them were divorced and single and not looking for long-term commitments. They also all seemed to really like his oral-sex technique. These were labiaplasty patients, with designer vaginas.

He was obsessed with testing out his creations and could report confidently that an unhooded clit with trimmed labia provided a more sensational shag for women. On the other hand, he personally missed the longer labia as they offered a bit more to suck on during oral sex.

Cons: If his wife found out he was shagging his patients, she would probably break his nose and report him to Sars for tax evasion. But he was actually more worried about one of his patients reporting him to the Health Professions Council for misconduct.

When the hour long session was up, the Duke had decided that for the next week he would try to restrict his sexual activity to his wife and the weekly whore. He agreed to take only one Dormicum at night and to restrict himself to three double whiskies on the rocks.

The Duke's fixation was predominately around sucking, but there were also anal and phallic fixations. Freud would have classified the Duke as having serious mental abnormalities, which were coming to the fore the more he drank and the more Dormicum he took. Jinny wondered what had gone wrong in his early development. The trigger had been his wife's affair with her trainer, but he had been shagging prostitutes long before that.

Either way, it was up to Jinny to help to get him onto a more even keel. Ethically, Jinny was only permitted to inform a spouse of what was going on if the other spouse was HIV positive.

She bade the Duke a friendly farewell at the door, encouraging him to keep himself on track, then walked through to reception to meet her next client, Aiden.

Aiden was 42, about six foot tall, with greying hair and a severe, no-nonsense look about him. He wore immaculate suits, smelt divine and chewed his fingernails nearly to the quick. He had a six-year-old son from a previous relationship whom he loved and adored. He had never married. He had come to see Jinny as he'd been dating a woman for a few months whom he had met online. He had enjoyed wining and dining her, spoiling her and travelling together. Then he learned she had been dating three different guys from the dating site simultaneously! He'd been gutted.

Jinny talked through a few options with him, but she had a feeling he probably wouldn't come to see her again. He really just needed a sounding board with whom to talk the situation through. Aiden was a lovely man, the kind of man who needed to be with a woman, who believed in romance, being faithful and looking after kids. He was pretty much everything Jinny had believed men to be when she had married Dylan. Back then she thought you fell in love, got married, had two children and then eased into a perfect, picket-fence life. But as one of her professors had once told her, "Yeah, the trouble with knights who come riding up in shining armour on a sturdy steed, is that the horse shits on your foot. No relationship is perfect. In fact they're pretty shitty in the end."

For Aiden's sake, Jinny hoped that he'd find a nice girl to share his life with. He seemed a lovely guy – he just had a few things he could work on when he was ready. At the end of their session, he thanked Jinny for her help and left.

Wow, she thought. What a diverse day. From a sex maniac deciding to scale his sex life down to his wife and his whore, to another male patient being shattered to find out that his new love had been three-timing him.

Another full and interesting day at work. It had also got an undeniable soupçon of friskiness going somewhere in the back of her mind! She called Ryder up.

"Ryder, I'd like to organise for us to sneak into my sister's place to use the Jacuzzi while she's away for the weekend. Are you keen?"

Ryder's reply was an unreserved Yes.

***

SHE ACTUALLY HAD no idea how the Jacuzzi even worked. And this was an outdoor one! In the end she had to ask him to come through the day before so they could figure the thing out. Ever the gentleman, he drove through to her sister's house to "come have a look". When not in glorious action, the Jacuzzi was a rather unattractive box overlooking the swimming pool. The two of them fiddled around with its settings, then filled it up, giggling like naughty kids. Once the Jacuzzi was filled, Ryder gave the heaters a test run and pronounced the hot tub ready for business. Then they put the cover back on and left.

Ryder had told his wife he was having a Sunday quadbiking session with "the boys". Little did he know that weekend events are the most frequently used ploy in the book, bike riding, quadbiking, cross-country events… Hang, one of Jinny's clients had even taken up paragliding just to have an excuse to be away. Sadly, he had crashed his paraglider, breaking both arms and ruining his extra-curricular sex life for eight weeks! Rider rolled up in his Audi 4X4 at Jinny's sister's place around 8am.

Just their luck, the weather had turned, and it was raining. Undaunted, Jinny had got up at 6am and the heaters were on. She'd read somewhere that they had hot tub parties in the snow in Colorado, so she wasn't going to let some Highveld rain spoil her plans.

She laid out a small Woolworths breakfast spread with some caramel yoghurt, croissants with cheese, blueberry and choc-chip muffins, and a fruit salad – sans pineapple, like Ryder preferred it. Ryder brought the champers and they enjoyed a merry breakfast in the kitchen. Pretty soon the bubbly had worked its magic and they stripped off in the kitchen, wrapped themselves in towels and made a dash for the hot tub through the rain with champers in hand.

It was so divine to be with Ryder in a home environment. Hotel rooms and health spas are fun, but being in a domestic setting just felt so much cosier. It felt real, not so illicit!

They lounged naked in the tub, sipping their champers, and enjoying the rain from the cosy, insulating warmth of the bubble jets. Steam rose from the Jacuzzi, mingling with the persistent drizzle. The jets made her feel light and of course it hid all the cellulite she didn't want Ryder to see. The warm water brought a pink flush to their skin. They swopped work stories and she gave him an update on the progress of her shambolic divorce. All the while they held hands and cuddled.

"How do the bubbles feel on your fanny? Do they turn you on?"

"Ha, ha! Not really. But watching your mighty fine equipment bobble around in the jets certainly does!"

He immediately took Jinny's hand and placed it on his dick.

"Do you want to play with me, Jinny?"

"Of course I want to play with you! Why do you think I brought you here?"

With that, she put down her champers, swung a leg across him and straddled his crotch. She gripped the back of his head, licked the side of his neck and nibbled on his earlobe as she grabbed his girth with her free hand.

Ryder had never been a gentle lover. At first Jinny had thought he must be angry with women, but over time she realised that he was just a hard lover, a bit rough, with almost zero foreplay technique. She always made sure she was properly turned on or had slapped on some lubricant before allowing him to penetrate her. Even then, she was seldom ready or wet enough for him. Sex in the water seemed romantic, but it had a nasty way of drying out her pussy and making penetration painful. And of course Ryder was a big boy. Still, in his own, old-fashioned way, he tried to be a considerate lover. He always asked if she was comfortable and he dearly wanted Jinny to come first. He would hold back until she was ready, but owing to the almost non-existent foreplay, it would take her longer to come than usual. She had to warm herself up quickly once he was inside her by playing with her clit. But that big, hard cock thrusting deep into her was a rare thrill. Such a full feeling. She could still feel Ryder inside her three days after they'd made love. And she liked that.

Arching his neck beneath her ministrations, Ryder reached down and pushed his fingers into her.

"Are you ready for me, Jinny. I'm feeling really hot!"

"Ha, ha! What kind of hot are you feeling? Are you hot for me or just feeling hot?"

"Jinny. I'm feeling hot..."

And he slumped back onto the edge of the Jacuzzi, gasping! Puce in the face!

"My God, Ryder, do you have a heart problem?"

Shit, Jinny thought. She worked with enough executives to know that many of them over the age of 50 had heart, cholesterol and blood sugar problems, why had she never asked him!

He was unable to speak. He just nodded. He was starting to slump into the water.

Fuck, fuck, fuck! The water was too hot! And he had heart problems! She should have realised this a long time ago. Sometimes it took ages to get him erect – the first sign of a heart problem. She worked with referrals from urologists every day. Why had she not picked this up?

Jinny forced herself to stay calm. She had already lost one husband – there was no way she was going to lose her best friend too.

"Okay, Ryder, let's get you out of this water. "Where are your heart pills? Did you take your heart pills this morning?"

"No. But I've been taking G4."

That's like taking Viagra. But it's not contra-indicated for patients with heart problems.

"How many did you take this morning?"

"Two."

"Good God Ryder! What were you thinking?"

"That I might get lucky!"

And he tried to make light of the situation!

"Right now, that's not very funny Ryder!"

But still, here he was, pink as a wet salmon and gasping for air in the hot tub. Okay. She needed to cool him down, and fast. With some feeble help from him she was able to lay him out on a towel in the rain.

He was still gasping like a fish out of water. But as least he was breathing.

"Ryder, where are your heart pills?"

"I left them at home on the kitchen counter"

"Do you have that emergency heart pill that you need to put under your tongue in your car?"

"No"

Shit, Christ, fuck! If worst came to worst, she would have to drive him home to get his pills. Who cares who would find out what they had been up to. She did care about Ryder and she definitely didn't want him to die!

Big boy that he was, Ryder weighed almost twice what she did. There was no way she was going to be able to get him into his car. She would need to call security to help her if needs be.

"Jinny will you resuscitate me if you need to?"

"Ryder, don't be silly now, man. Of course I will! You're my best friend."

"Do you think you can still resuscitate my willy?"

She couldn't help chuckling at that, potential heart attack notwithstanding. The two of them laughed, clinging to each other in the rain like two drenched rats.

"Seriously, Ryder, this is not funny."

"I know. I feel so silly here in the rain. Have you seen that TV programme on 101 Stupid Ways To Die?"

"Yes. And you're not going to make it 102, ha, ha! It's okay my sweetheart. I'm with you. I'm not going to leave you on your own. We're going to sit here in the rain until you feel well enough to get up and go inside."

It took him a good fifteen minutes to stop gasping like a landed fish. Then he was able to slowly get up and they wobbled inside together like an old couple. Jinny wrapped Ryder in a dry towel. There was probably a short window period between him overheating and when he started to shiver with cold.

"How about that coffee and a nice chocolate muffin, Jinny? I'm famished!"

They sat side by side, wrapped in towels, sipped their coffee and ate their muffins, and slowly the world eased back onto its axis. The static of horror that had crackled in the air only half an hour ago slowly dissipated and things returned to normal.

"Are you feeling a bit better? Because your gasping goldfish look is a bit alarming!" They laughed, and he had a good sense of humour about his wobble, but she could see he was tired. He needed to get that heart pill ASAP.

"Hun, are you well enough to drive home, or do you want me to drive you?"

"No, I'm okay. I can drive."

"Well, maybe you should go now, before you start feeling ill. Let's get you dressed."

As she closed the door behind him and began scanning the premises for evidence of their aborted tryst, she gave a deep sigh. Merde! What a disaster. But more than anything, she was just so relieved that Ryder was okay.

***

JINNY ARRIVED AT her office on Monday at 8am and called him up to check that he was okay. Ryder was still in the land of the living, so she logged on and began wading through her emails.

Here was one from Aiden the new patient, thanking her for the consultation and informing her that he would not be coming back. A slightly odd email, as most patients who don't like what you have to say, just don't come back. We're all adults here – no need for the big farewell email! Perhaps since he was an attorney, he felt the need to email. She decided to call him up.

"Good morning, Aiden. I got your email…"

"Ja."

"I just wanted to check, um… You must feel quite strongly about not coming back if you felt the need to send an email. Most patients just never return. May I ask why you wanted to make it so, er, official?"

"Ja, I suppose it is quite formal. The thing is… Well, Jinny, it's quite simple. When I was in our session, I suddenly felt I would like to kiss you. And I just don't think that, with you being my counsellor, would be entirely appropriate."

Now that was a first. But hey, there'd been a lot of firsts in the past two years. She was getting used to it. Jinny was caught off guard for only a few seconds, then she couldn't help laughing.

"Sorry, I didn't mean to laugh. I'm just… I'm blushing – that's quite flattering. I can understand why you'd want to end counselling sessions if you felt like kissing your counsellor. But how do you know I wouldn't have liked it?"

She could hear from the brief silence on the phone that she'd caught him off guard too.

"Look, Aiden, I appreciate your honesty and your… integrity. Thank you for letting me know why you don't want to come back. But if you really feel that way, and you'd like to go out for a drink some time let me know. I'd definitely be interested!"

They hung up simultaneously.

***

HER CONSULTANCY HAD suffered badly since Justin and that cow of his had sent that fraudulent complaint out. They had pretty much succeeded in alienating all the websites she'd been listed on. Now she needed to diversify her consultancy if she was going to survive. She'd been racking her brains about it during all of her sleepless nights. Finally she'd come up with an idea. She would submit a proposal to companies who had excellent corporate social investment programmes. The idea was to get them to support something she would call Safe Spaces. Safe spaces was about freeing children from domestic violence and working to prevent future violence.

Studies show that there are adult and child victims in 30 to 60 per cent of families experiencing domestic violence (Appel and Holden, 1998; Edleson, 1999; Jaffe and Wolfe, 1990).

Childhood problems associated with exposure to domestic violence fall into three primary categories:

Behavioural, social, and emotional problems High levels of aggression, anger, hostility, oppositional behaviour, and disobedience; fear, anxiety, withdrawal, and depression; poor peer-, sibling-, and social relationships and low self-esteem.

Cognitive and attitudinal problems Low cognitive functioning, poor school performance, lack of conflict-resolution skills, limited problem-solving skills, pro-violent attitudes, and belief in rigid gender stereotypes and male privilege.

Long-term problems High levels of adult depression and trauma symptoms and increased tolerance for, and use of violence in adult relationships.

Children's risk levels and reactions to domestic violence exist on a continuum where some children show enormous resilience while others show significant maladjustment (Carlson, 2000; Edleson, 1999; Hughes, Graham-Bermann & Gruber, 2001).

Factors such as social competence, intelligence, high self-esteem, outgoing temperament, strong sibling and peer relationships, and a supportive relationship with an adult, can help protect children from the adverse effects of exposure to domestic violence.

Nature of the violence Children who witness frequent, severe forms of violence or fail to observe their caretakers resolving conflict may undergo more distress than children who witness fewer incidences of physical violence and experience positive interactions between their caregivers.

Age of the child Younger children appear to exhibit higher levels of emotional and psychological distress than older children. Age-related differences might result from older children's more fully developed cognitive abilities to understand the violence and select various coping strategies to alleviate upsetting symptoms.

These children are psychologically and often physically scarred by their experiences. They struggle to concentrate at school, battle to build good relationships and have problems participating in society. The long-term result of growing up, plagued by fear and insecurity is low self-esteem. Often this results in adults who lack empathy and who perpetuate the intergenerational cycle of habitual violence and abuse.

South Africa has one of the best constitutions for children in the world, but an inability to implement the law, owing to a lack of funds, resources and hands-on support for victims of violence. The impact of random violence or ongoing abuse often goes unnoticed.

Jinny's Safe Spaces concept was designed to assist with the implementation of the law by developing cross-system protocols and partnerships to ensure coordinated services and responses to families. Institutional and societal changes can only begin when an expansive network of service providers integrates their expertise, resources, and services to eliminate domestic violence in their communities. Thus, Safe Spaces could collaborate to achieve a shared goal of freeing victims from violence and working to prevent future violence.

She wanted to show her proposal to Ryder – he was the only friend she felt safe enough with to show it to. He knew what had happened to her…

***

JINNY HAD ALWAYS wanted to be a sexologist because she wanted to help people recover from abuse. Oddly, she seldom analysed her own sexuality and her behaviour. But now, as she started putting together her proposal for Safe Spaces, she started to wonder if her current sexual behaviour had anything to do with the abuse she had experienced as a child, and at the hands of her second husband.

Maybe she was suffering from attachment disorder. As a counsellor, she knew full well there was no cure for it. So it was best just to deal with it and keep her mouth shut. After all, patients didn't come to see her because they were interested in her life and how she was doing. Patients came to see her because she was good at what she did and because they wanted help in their lives. They paid her to help them, they weren't at all interested in her issues.

Jinny liked to help people. It was just in her nature.

As a little girl, before her life changed when she was ten, she could remember always wanting to help anyone who was hurt or in pain. When she was about five she had overheard her mom saying she was going to kill all the snails in the garden. The next morning she had woken up at 4am, rushed into the garden and collected all the snails. She'd put them in a box with some grass and hidden them under the bed. The trouble started when Jinny came home from school. She discovered that the snails had escaped from the box and were now crawling all over her walls. Of course she didn't mind – she was just happy that they were okay.

Jinny knew that even if she had not been abused as a child she still would have chosen counselling. But being abused had definitely led her to take a highly specific counselling route.

***

THE DUKE WAS coming in for a consultation and Jinny wondered what he had been up to in the past week, and if he had managed to restrain himself.

When he arrived, the Duke seemed jittery. Jinny gently enquired how much he'd been drinking.

"Jinny, I fear I've got myself into a spot of trouble."

"Oh dear. What kind of trouble?"

"Well, my wife went through my Blackberry. She found the SMSes between me and one of my patients."

"Is that awkward?"

"To say the least. The SMSes were to thank her for the beautiful blowjob she gave me the last time she was in town. Then there's the one where I say how much I love her and how I'm considering leaving my wife for her."

"It sounds like you've got yourself into more than a spot of bother, Bushmore."

"Well, yes. The whole situation is a tad troublesome."

"Alright, so how did you handle the situation?"

"Well, I told my wife that I've been seeing you for counselling because I've not been able to get over her swallowing her personal trainer's cum. I told her that you said I should get a divorce. Needless to say she got herself into a Tasmanian Devil of a rage and now she's gonna be coming after you…"

"What?"

"…but it's okay. Isn't that what I pay you for? To handle situations like this?"

Jinny felt herself go cold. He had sold her out! She had gone out of her way to help the Duke, to steer him towards getting his relationship problems with his wife sorted out. And now, when push came to shove, he'd thrown his wife a red herring and told her, no, Jinny said I should get a divorce. Rather that than actually coming clean with what he was really doing –compulsively shagging half the women he knew. Here it was again! That rich boy sense of entitlement!

"That's what I pay you for. To handle situations like this."

Jinny knew he was lost. It would be three to five years before someone found him "sleeping like the dead" in his bed. She felt really sad about it – she'd hoped the Duke would have the strength, the gumption, to sort out his dysfunctional life. But instead of sorting his stuff out, he'd fed her to his Tasmanian devil.

"Bushmore, we need to be clear on a few things. As a doctor yourself, you must be fully aware that you're protected by client confidentiality. So even if your wife did call me and ask what the hell was going on, I wouldn't be able to disclose anything to her."

"I know, what a relief."

"I think you're also aware that you have now compromised your counselling sessions with me and that I will need to refer you to another specialist."

"I know… Look… I'm so sorry for the trouble I've caused you, Jinny."

And with that, he stood up and left.

Crap! What a horrible thing to do - to use your counsellor as a scapegoat for your own misbehaviour. Tragically, this kind of thing was not uncommon. It happened to every counsellor at least once in their careers, and usually with patients whom you go out of your way to assist. The same people you go out of your way to help are the very same people who betray and crush you.

Damn it all to hell, Jinny thought. She was really disappointed in the Duke. But more than that, she was going to have to find herself an attorney now. The Duke was going to be spinning a long line of lies that she would not even be able to address as she was bound by client confidentially. Now he said that his wife was going to be coming after her – no doubt with him funding all the legal action. He'd probably also be fuelling the fire with his wife and making sure that she became distracted and obsessed with bringing this "home-wrecking counsellor" down. That way, he'd be able to carry on with his shenanigans in peace. He had more than enough money to fund her rage about his indiscretion and Jinny's "divorce recommendation".

The first attorney who came to mind was Aiden. He was no longer a patient of Jinny's as he'd officially "fired her". But he was a jolly good attorney and since he'd only come for one session and they hadn't seen each other in months, she should be able to approach him with this problem. She was sure as hell going to need legal assistance with this. And while she was looking at worst-case scenarios, she'd probably need to contact her counsellors' board to tell them to expect a call from the disgruntled spouse of a patient.

Besides this latest drama, Jinny also wanted to talk through Safe Spaces with Aiden. He specialised in commercial law and perhaps he had a few corporate contacts she could approach with the proposal.

She met with Aiden a week later and ran through the devilish-spouse problem she was anticipating as well as the Safe Spaces proposal. Aiden said he'd be happy to assist with the spouse if needs be, and he thought that Safe Spaces was an excellent proposal. He suggested that Jinny set up a meeting at his office with a few of the corporates she knew, so they could brainstorm the idea further. She was excited about his feedback. It was a validation of her ideas and her judgement. As they got up to leave the coffee shop, he seemed to hesitate.

"Have you got anything on now?" he asked.

"No, why?"

"Would you like to follow me back to my house for a sundowner?"

Why not! It had been a hectic week, and a sundowner sounded like a fine idea.

Jinny followed Aiden home for that sundowner. It turned out he had a beautiful, big home in an exclusive estate with huge concrete statue of a classical nude at his front entrance. It would've made a better water feature beside a pond. The furniture was dark and heavy, with library shelves filled with books. The whole place looked a bit like a museum, in fact it kind of reminded her of that DStv series The Librarians. It was unusual décor for a bachelor pad, but at least she wouldn't have to climb through the bathroom window to escape from his dodgy décor. And at 40, he wasn't a young bachelor anyway!

"So, Jinny, what do you think of my place?"

"It's lovely, Aiden. It looks a bit like a museum, but it's home to you and that's what counts."

The bedroom had a massive, low "Shag me, Baby" couch and a huge flat-screen TV. It lead onto a spacious balcony. Now this was looking more like a bachelor pad!

Aiden poured a Coke Lite for Jinny, and a glass of red wine for himself, then they ambled out onto the balcony. They sat chatting, sipping their drinks and watched the sun go down.

"Would you like to stay for a bite to eat? We could watch a DVD or something?"

She readily agreed – if only because she was curious to see that massive TV in action. He phoned out for pizzas and they moved into the main-bedroom lounge area and snuggled up for the movie. The movie itself was dreadful, some typically over-the-top disaster movie, but it felt good snuggling up next to him. She felt comfortable in Aiden's space. Even though he seemed so serious, he actually had a lovely, quiet, self-deprecating humour.

"What is it with you, Jinny?" he grinned. "The first time I saw you for a consultation, you told me I needed to exercise more and lose a bit of weight. And today you tell me my house looks like a museum. Am I to assume I'm a fat old fart?"

He tried to keep a straight face, but they both burst out laughing.

"Well, now that you put it that way, it doesn't sound like such a nice thing to say, but you are looking a lot more toned. Are you spending more time on that treadmill?"

He chuckled.

"And while we're criticising, you should consider getting rid of that concrete statue in your entrance hall…"

Aiden laughed out loud.

"That happens to be a very expensive sculpture!"

"Oh," Jinny warmed to her topic. "Well I think they may have ripped you off at the art gallery. It just looks like any old concrete statue to me."

They were both chuckling as Aiden leaned in and kissed her.

He had lovely, full lips. Eminently kissable. She responded with enthusiasm. He eased his tongue into Jinny's mouth. It tasted cosy and warm. He had a homecoming feeling to him. She wanted more. She moved closer. This was so simple. There was no anger or fear around Aiden. She just felt safe. Aiden took her hand and moved it down the front of his pants onto his dick. Hard, beautiful and enticing. But something made her stop.

She couldn't do this with Aiden. She knew how gutted he'd been when he'd found out his girlfriend had been three-timing him. She couldn't be the next one to let him down. Aiden wasn't a cheat, he wasn't some married guy having an affair on the side. He was a steady, decent man. She hadn't quite told him that she was still married, in dire financial trouble, and that she was a serial monogamist, only loyal to the guy she was shagging on that day. And she certainly hadn't shared her psychological issues about men and how every one she'd known had proven himself a prize, cheating arsehole. She really didn't want to entangle this lovely man in her dysfunction. He deserved better.

Jinny stopped kissing him and pulled back slightly.

"Aiden, thank you for the lovely sundowners. And for the movie. But it's time for me to go."

She got up and grabbed her handbag.

"Would you be kind enough to let me out?"

Looking surprised and slightly dumbstruck, he cleared his throat a few times and stammered, "Of course."

Shit, she thought on the drive home. He must think I'm a real cock-teasing bitch. But she just couldn't go any further knowing full well what a decent guy Aiden was – the kind of guy who needs a fairy tale romance and a princess.

***

THERE WAS STILL the awkward issue of the proposal. Until she'd let her passions get the better of her, she'd needed Aiden's help with pitching it. So once she'd calmed down, Jinny called him up at work and thanked him again for the lovely evening. She apologised for rushing off and asked if it would still be in order for them to meet with some corporates to brainstorm the Safe Spaces proposal.

Aiden said yes, with pleasure, and they set a date.

Then she called Ryder and asked if she could forward him the proposal to read and whether he'd be prepared to meet at Aiden's office to brainstorm the pitch with her.

Ryder, apart from being her best friend, was also her most loyal supporter. If she was on the radio or on TV or in magazines, he always made the effort to watch, listen or read the coverage. He was a busy executive who had taken the time to actually get to know her, and she placed a lot of value on his advice and ideas.

Then she called up Christiaan and asked if he'd be prepared to read the proposal and then brainstorm the idea. He was also in. Things were looking good.

It was three weeks before she could get Ryder, Aiden and Chris together in the same room. She was excited to share her idea with these high-powered, intelligent, successful men. She wanted to hear their views and ideas on the proposal. She really wanted to do something meaningful to improve children's lives – but she also needed a good break. Maybe this could be the game changer that got big corporates involved in fighting abuse, and also put her consultancy back on its feet.

She managed to book a boardroom at Aiden's law firm. Everyone arrived on time and the pace of the meeting was fast. Everyone had something to say or add or an angle to suggest that she hadn't thought of before. Their ideas were fresh and practical – the kind of input that develops an idea into reality. Safe Spaces was going to happen.

Then, in the middle of the meeting, Jinny had a moment of clarity. She sat back and realised the full implications of setting up this meeting. What an incredibly wild, stupid chance she was taking? She had been intimately involved on some level with every single one of these men! She looked around the room at them all furiously brainstorming the concept and helping her with her idea. There was something sexy about that focus, that intensity. And although two of these chaps were unfaithful cheats, they weren't bad men. Quite the opposite, they were good men who were going out of their way to help her. Perhaps in the past they had taken advantage of her vulnerable situation. They were opportunistic hound-dogs, sure, but they had by no means abused her. She had been a willing participant. In fact, you could possibly make a case for her having abused them!

Jinny started to feel incredibly ashamed of herself. She wasn't too worried about Aiden – she had only kissed him, after all. But she was really worried about Ryder finding out about Christiaan and Aiden.

Chris had been her friend for years. He liked pussy – there was no getting away from that – but he had always played along with Jinny and done everything she wanted. "I want you to get down on your knees and lick me until I cum…" And he had done it! He was an opportunistic, unfaithful slut, but at the end of the day he wasn't a bad guy – just an extremely unfaithful one. He was duty bound to his wife and he loved his kids to bits. He was kind and softly spoken and highly intelligent. He had always made her feel good about herself. Jinny knew she didn't love him, nor did she even respect him that much. He was a friend who had turned into a friend with benefits for a while.

And then there was Ryder. Dear, sweet, wonderful Ryder, who had the ability to make her more angry and upset than anyone she had ever met. But he also had that uncanny way of getting to the source of things, being able to see through to the vulner-able side of Jinny that she liked to keep so well hidden.

Ryder had mentioned on several occasions things like "You have so much love to give. You are worth so much more." She was fond of Ryder, but over time she had also come to really respect him. That was a first – she had never genuinely respected a man before.

It took an incredible man to take the time to get to know and understand someone and then to walk alongside them and guide them. To try to help them find what's right for them, what would make them happy.

The greatest love is unconditional, uncontrolling, unselfish. It holds no records of wrongs, accepts a person's weaknesses and focuses on a person's strengths. Ryder's love was all that and more. He found joy in watching Jinny do well, and wanted her to succeed.

Ryder was a good man and it was an honour to be loved and supported by someone like him. It gave her joy to love Ryder back. Jinny had only realised how much she actually cared for Ryder when he was gasping like a goldfish out of water after she'd nearly killed him in that hot Jacuzzi.

With Ryder it wasn't just the sex. Jinny knew that for sure, because his foreplay was rudimentary and he was a really hard lover. It was the other things that set him apart from any other man she'd ever known. He'd taken the time to get to know her. No matter how busy his days were, he always made time for her. He always took her calls, or sent an SMS to say he was in a meeting and would call her back. He always asked after the kids. He was seldom late for their breakfast and lunch dates and he had never stood her up. He seldom took calls on his mobile when they were together, unless it was his wife or his kids calling. He always dedicated the time that they had to her. Ryder was like her big piece of decadent chocolate cake – sweet, rich and a special indulgence. He had never shouted at her, or manhandled her. Although, she had felt a bit vulnerable when he'd held her wrists and tried to calm her down that once. But once he'd learned about what happened to her, he had never done that again.

In fact, Ryder had gone out of his way to get her to talk about the things that worried her. The only time Ryder had ever got angry, he had said, "Jinny, you have offended me." She'd said, "Well, you have offended me too. I think that was horrible. I am angry with you."

That had led to their three-week cold war, when they hadn't seen each other. But even then, he'd still SMSed and called to check if she was okay.

That was the only way Ryder ever reprimanded her. He just excused himself from her – and that was the worst punishment of all, because she loved laughing and talking and spending time with him. She loved simple pleasures like holding his hand.

And he really was funny too, without really realising he was funny. Like the time he had gone through what Jinny thought was his Manopause/Midlife-crisis year. He had bought himself a two-door Aston Martin. He'd been so incredibly proud of his car and had come to show it off. He'd come bouncing out of the car wearing the worst saggy, baggy, blue jeans imaginable. A garment that didn't match the car at all. Then he had gone through the trying-to-look-a-bit-younger phase, when he'd gone for laser treatment on his face "to get rid of all the cancer spots". He'd chosen this time to go back to driving with his hood down and got his face sunburnt all over again. Then he'd settled down a bit and bought himself a more practical Audi 4X4 that covered his bald head and protected his face.

Jinny's fondest memory of his Aston Martin midlife crisis had been when she and her friend Kalin had given Ryder a car-christening party. Kalin was stunning, with long, beautiful, strong legs that went on forever. She was always keen to join a party, so they had both got dolled up and had arranged to meet Ryder for Friday sundowners. Then they'd convinced him to take them for a spin in his new car.

At the end of it, when Ryder had parked the convertible and helped Jinny and Kalin out of the car, they had each taken a "wing" and walked him into the restaurant like he was The Man. After dinner, they had progressed to gate-crash a private party where the three of them had danced for hours. She'd been surprised to see that Ryder was actually a good dancer. They had topped the evening off sitting by the hotel pool sipping drinks till 1am. On the way back, as they cruised sedately down the highway with the hood down – Ryder never drove recklessly, ever! – a group of students in a clapped-out little car had wound down their windows and screamed, "You're one lucky guy!" Ryder had almost burst with pride. He'd carried on looking straight ahead, but said, "Oh, that's so nice." Then he'd turned to Jinny and chuckled. When they got back to Monte, Jinny and Kalin had instructed Ryder to park and then get out of the car and walk off a ways so he could get a good view of them by his car.

"Take a car-christening picture," they'd screamed, as they both whipped off their tops! It was such a happy evening.

She already had an entire memory bank filled with happy things that she and Ryder had done together.

Ryder had met her at what Jinny had thought was the lowest point of her life. But now, sitting around the boardroom table with her three love interests, these three conquests of hers, she realised that today was her lowest point. And like a bolt from the blue, she realised that somehow she had come to love Ryder.

OMG, Jinny what are you thinking? How could you possibly be in love with Ryder? He is married. What makes you think he'd be loyal to you if you were involved with him? Ryder has always made it clear that he wants you to find a decent man to love and be married to. He has always been clear on that – and that he would never leave his ailing wife.

You are nothing more than an interesting project to Ryder, one of his little staffie dogs that he likes to look after in his back garden. Note to self, Jinny – the back garden! You are not a front-of-house person to Ryder. And you've behaved like an absolute harlot. You've never met his family, he's never introduced you to his friends… You've barely even been at the same social gatherings. You are nothing more than an interesting and isolated project in his mind.

Blissfully unaware of the crisis going on in Jinny's mind, the guys continued the meeting, all coming up with fascinating, dynamic ideas for Jinny's proposal. She appreciated all of their input, but she couldn't end the meeting soon enough. As soon she could, she wrapped things up. She thanked the gentlemen for their ideas and their time and asked Aiden to escort Christiaan out. She wanted to have a word with Ryder on her own.

"Thanks so much for coming, Ryder, I appreciate your input so much. Can I stand you to a cup of coffee?"

"Of course. I'd love one."

They walked out of the office together and into the lift, where they chatted quietly, and held hands all the way down to the ground floor.

Ryder was sincerely impressed with her proposal and they discussed it for a while. Then he had to rush off to another meeting. The coffee date hadn't achieved much.

Jinny sat alone at the table in the coffee shop. She ordered another tea and then asked the waiter to bring her a shot of whisky on ice. She sat sipping her tea with alternate slugs of whisky, gradually coming to the realisation that this meeting had probably been the culmination of three years of her own dysfunctional behaviour. Not to mention the lowest point in her life.

Fuck, she thought. And not in a good way! How had she got herself into such a mess? She really needed to get help – even if it was just an attachment disorder she was suffering from, she really needed to seek professional help now. Her own hatred and anger at cheating, abusive men had turned her into an abusive, cheating woman. How did the saying go? The abused frequently becomes the abuser or as her proposal said, "Children see and children do."

OMG, she thought. I am such a damn mess! How the hell can I be counselling people when my own life is falling apart in such a big way?

***

THE DUKE'S WIFE was on the rampage and as Jinny had anticipated, it was only a matter of time before she called her. She threatened to defame her in some way or report her to the counselling board. Luckily for the Duke, the more time his wife spent trying to ferret out what was going on, the more time he had to go back to his old ways of shagging prostitutes and patients. As Jinny had intuitively thought when she had first met the Duke, this was the dysfunctional game they played with each other. But it was far more entrenched and far more wicked than Jinny had initially realised. There is an excellent book, The Games People Play: The Psychology of Human Relationships by psychiatrist Eric Berne, published in 1964, that describes the kind of games that the two of them were playing, almost word for word. It describes both functional and dys-functional social interactions.

Jinny knew it would get to a stage where she'd have to ask Aiden to step in and sort the problem out. Jinny was bound by client confidentiality and was unable to disclose to the Duke's wife what he had been up to. She knew that she was going to take the fall for the Duke and that the little ponce was quite happy for this to happen. On the grand scale of things, who was she really, anyway? He was rich and successful, and money could buy you just about anything. It could ensure that you got away with just about anything too.

This was a time when she really needed her wits about her. There were shades of Justin and Nora's vendetta about this. And that had brought her to the brink of a break-down, and hadn't been resolved yet.

Now with this vengeful wife on the warpath, Jinny needed to get her mind in order. It was her only survival tool. She needed to finally and ultimately sort out her psychological issues, or she would be unable to deal with the very real, practical threats to her survival.

To do that, she needed the best psychologist available. One whom she had always admired, was high-profile forensic profiler Jonathan Gordon. He was highly respected in the field, and he'd featured in magazines and newspapers. He seemed level headed, with an in-depth knowledge of abuse. Maybe he would be able to shed some light on Jinny's life and why she was doing the strange things she was doing. Maybe, just maybe, Jonathan could help her. She went onto his website and booked an appointment.

Part of her was scared to go and see Jonathan Gordon. What if he told her – as she had suspected all along – that she had an attachment disorder and that nobody could help her? Jinny felt nervous, sick and trapped all at the same time.

She could completely relate to how her patients felt the first time they came in to see her for a consultation. It is really difficult to tell someone the full truth about what you have been up to but Jinny was desperate. She didn't care any longer if someone knew everything about her. She wanted to get help and she wanted to get better. She wanted to get her kids back and her life on track. She had researched Jonathan. He was an Orthodox Jew with a wife and three children. Jinny wanted to see him because ultimately this is what she wanted for herself – a respectful husband, a loving father, and functional family. Half of her suspected that with Jonathan being an orthodox Jew, he'd kick her right out of his consultancy rooms when she told him what a dreadfully wicked, wayward and bad person she was. But with all the forensic criminal work he did, he'd surely dealt with far worse things. Jinny had not quite got to the point of being a criminal, but she was not exactly certain that, if she met St. Peter at the Pearly gates, he would let her in!

She would just try to be as matter of fact as possible. She arrived for their session, and as Jonathan closed the door to his consulting room, she felt afraid.

"Can you please leave the door open? I'm feeling scared."

"Of course."

He got up and opened the door.

Jonathan was like a big, huggable teddy bear. He spoke gently and he had a way about him that put her at ease. He had a massive box of Gary Player tissues on a side table by the patients' couch. She couldn't help laughing.

"Wow, people must do a lot of crying here if you need such huge tissues!"

"Yes," he smiled. "We deal with serious issues here. How can I help you, Jinny?"

"Well," Jinny said, "I am a counsellor and I love working with people and helping them put their lives back in order. But the reality is that I am a mess. I don't know if anyone can help me really, but I have been doing really stupid, dysfunctional, self-destructive things. I need to stop doing what I am doing, but I don't know why I am doing what I am doing. I have read up on my behaviours and I have come to the conclusion that I have an attachment disorder… which is scary, because I know there is no help for me if I do."

Jonathan leaned forward.

"Okay, Jinny. First things first. You know full well, being a counsellor, that the biggest mistake you can make is to try to self-diagnose. So why don't you tell me what has been going on in your life."

"Well, where should I start, Jonathan? At the beginning of the story or at the end?"

"Wherever you would like to start."

Jinny decided to start at the beginning.

"I was adopted at the age of three. I went from being an only child and all alone, to being one of five children. I remember feeling afraid of my mom a lot. She shouted a lot and I was always trying to be good and to keep out of her way so she wouldn't scream at me.

"Things seemed to settle down for a while, and then my stepfather started molesting me when I was 10. This went on until I was 13, when my parents got divorced. I was sent to a girls' boarding school in Johannesburg. I matriculated as a pretty average student, and I married my first love when I was 21. He was ten years older than I was.

"I really just wanted to have a little family to myself, my own little family to love. I wanted to create my own perfect, picket-fence life, because the Lord himself knows I had an interrupted childhood.

"Everything went along fine for a while and then just after my little son was born, my husband killed himself and left me on my own with a tiny baby. I couldn't cope and moved back to my mom and her next husband. He was socially inept, but a kind and stable man. I stayed for a while, but I still wanted to have my own family and my own life. I met and married a man who turned out to be really abusive. I had a daughter with my second husband. I had always really wanted two children. Then there were several years of living in an environment that felt like daily Chinese torture. But despite that, I managed to build up a successful counselling practice. I really enjoy helping people.

"I finally left him. But in leaving him, I lost everything I owned. I lost my main source of income and financial stability and landed up having to move both of my children to the Cape. I had always wanted to have a big boy and a tiny little girl. God was merciful and gave me what I asked for. Since then I have desperately been trying to get my life back in order, but my estranged husband is frustrating the legal processes and messing me around financially. So I'm still trying to close this chapter of my life. I'm sleeping on my friend's couch, because I don't even have my own home any more. I can't start the next chapter of my life because I seem to be perpetuating the abuse in my life and making a mess of things.

"I have got myself into a situation with two married men. The one, I genuinely respect and love, but the relationship is absolutely stuffed because he is married and will never leave his wife. I would never respect him if he did leave his wife because she has been dying for a long time. I am an absolutely worthless rat and I don't know why I have been behaving this way, but I need help to sort myself out. Every morning when I wake up I feel like taking out a butcher's knife and running full-force into a brick wall to drive it through my heart. Just so I can end this all. But my kids believe in me; they believe I can sort his out. I have no idea how I am going to sort it out, though… I just… I don't know."

Jinny stopped, caught her breath and looked at Jonathan.

"Wow, Jinny. You have had a really rough time. How do you feel?"

"I feel like a dirty, rotten hobo. That's how I feel."

"Do you feel sad, Jinny?"

"Yes. Pretty much all the time."

"Do you feel hopeless?"

"Yes, all the time."

"Do you try to control things all the time, because you feel out of control on the inside all the time?"

"Yes."

"Do you get yourself into relationships, but as soon as the person wants to be your special person you push them away? And you choose never to see them again?"

"Oh, yes. Oh, yes."

"As much as you want to be in a relationship, does the thought of being in a relationship make you feel anxious and trapped?"

"Yes."

"Do you think that maybe you're choosing to be involved with married men on purpose? Perhaps so that they're not in a position to claim you or control you as their own?"

"Yes."

"Do you feel angry, Jinny?"

"Yes."

"Do you have night and day sweats?"

"Oh, my God, yes. It's so irritating!"

"Do you suffer from insomnia?"

"Yes."

"Do you feel anxious all the time?"

"Yes."

"Do you have a feeling of impending doom? Do you feel that the world is an unsafe place?"

"Yes"

"Do you have anyone in your life who you feel you can trust?"

"Yes"

"Who, Jinny?"

"Ryder. I can trust Ryder."

"And who is Ryder?"

"Ryder is one of the married guys."

"Okay."

"Is this where you're going to tar and feather me, Jonathan?"

"No, Jinny. It sounds like you have had a really rough time and you've done some pretty wild things. But you are able to recover from this."

"Please tell me what's wrong with me! Or is there no help for me? Am I just stuffed in the head?"

"Jinny, you are probably suffering from Stockholm Syndrome."

"What? Are you sure, Jonathan? It's not like I'm in love with my estranged husband. I don't even have feelings of empathy and sympathy or any positive feelings toward him. If he was standing in front of me choking, I would count the minutes until he suffocated. I would not even bother to go to his funeral, but I would feel incredibly relieved if he died."

"Jinny, I want you to pause for a minute. I know this may be difficult to absorb, because you've barely mentioned that you have been a victim of abuse… or been able to express how you actually feel! You've been sitting here telling me the details as if you are a third party regurgitating a story. But you have been unable to tell me how you feel."

"Because I am not a victim, Jonathan."

"Yes, you are!"

"But I don't want to be a victim!"

"Listen, I know you're a very strong, very brave girl, Jinny!"

"Well then why do I feel like such a rat?"

"Let me explain Jinny. Let me explain…"

And he did so. In his slightly academic, thoroughly educated manner, drawing on the well of his vast experience, he analysed the factors that had brought Jinny to her current situation. It was like someone explaining a riddle you've been trying to solve for your entire life…

"As a child, you were raped repeatedly by your adoptive father. Your survival depended on this man.

"In order for Stockholm Syndrome to occur in any given situation, you need three things:
• An uneven power relationship, where the captor dictates what the prisoner can and can't do.
• The threat of death or physical injury to the captive.
• A self-preservation instinct on the part of the prisoner.

"You also need the prisoner to believe that he or she can't escape. This means the captor sets all the rules. And the prisoner is isolated. So he or she has no outside view of the captor. This is what leads to Stockholm syndrome.

So there's a traumatic event, and a woman finds herself held captive by a man. She is abused – physically, sexually and verbally – and has trouble thinking straight. According to the captor, escape is not an option. So her only chance of survival is obedience.

As time goes on, obedience alone may become less of a guarantee of survival. A change in the captor's mood could have harmful consequences. So, in order to survive, she tries to work out what might set off her captor's violence. In this way, she gets to know her captor.

Also, if the captor shows a bit of kindness, he feels like her saviour. Even young Anne Frank famously wrote that the Nazis were "ultimately good". But they ultimately caused her death. In traumatic, life-threatening circumstances, the slightest act of kindness – or the sudden absence of violence – seems like a sign of friendship. The prisoner clings to this for dear life.

So the captor gradually seems less threatening – more an instrument for survival and protection than one of harm. The prisoner starts deluding him or herself. In order to survive psychologically as well as physically – to lessen the unimaginable stress of the situation – the prisoner comes to truly believe that the captor is her friend, that he will not kill her. She starts to believe that they can help each other "get out of this mess".

"Jinny, you were only ten when the sexual assaults started happening. You probably had only just started going through puberty…"

"Well, yes Jonathan. But what does that have to do with the way I'm behaving now? That happened years ago! My parents got divorced, I went to a private school and I got on with my life."

"Was your family, or were you, ever counselled, Jinny?"

"No, my family wasn't counselled. I went for one or two sessions with a therapist when I was about 14. But that was absolutely useless, and I never went back."

"What were you like as a child? Were you a rebellious child? Did you show contempt for authority figures? Do you have a silent anger inside you that sometimes bubbles up like a volcano, but you never let it out?"

"Yes, I have to say… Yes."

"Jinny, you have had one massive trauma after another in your life. Being adopted and put into a family when you were three, being attacked for years, getting married and your husband committing suicide. Then getting remarried and being beaten and abused, losing your home and your money and having to send your kids to your mom and stepdad… And now you're desperately trying to make money so that you can fulfil your dream of having your own home and a happy little family…

"The last three years of your life have been what we call acting out – in essence, you have relived being held hostage as a child, but this time you have been calling the shots. I don't agree or condone your getting involved with married men. But although it may seem like you've been rushing off the rails and your behaviour has been wild, it's been your mind's own way of trying to recover from a series of very traumatic events in your life. In a way, you've let that angry volcano out because your adopted father held you down and told you to shhhhh… To this day, you have been unable to voice how you felt. So your mind chose to physically act things out.

"Oh", Jinny said. "Well this is absolutely unexpected. I really did think I had an attachment disorder "

"Your two hours are up, Jinny. But I would like to meet with you next week so we can start the process of getting you back on track… If that's what you would really like to do…"

Jinny wanted to cry and scream simultaneously, but mostly she just felt tired. She felt like she could sleep for a thousand years. She was relieved that it wasn't an attachment disorder, and to know that actually, just maybe, Jonathan could help her get onto an even keel.

***

RYDER CALLED TO ask how her session had gone. She said it had been interesting and she would tell him about it some time. But not today.

"Okay, Jinny. Whenever you're ready to talk about it, I'm here. But I am glad that you're seeing Jonathan, I've heard a lot of good things about him."

She really wasn't feeling well. It was probably emotional distress and having to talk again about what had happened to her as a child. But she was getting severe stomach pains with this weird burning sensation down her right leg. Perhaps it was time that she took herself off for a gynae check-up. She booked an appointment with a gynae who came well recommended. Some guy who was apparently excellent at keyhole surgery – not that she anticipated being operated on any time soon. But here she was, nearing her 40s. That was when women usually started to have female problems. And she had been having those night and day sweats. She may need to have a hysterectomy.

The gynae had a lovely bedside manner. He did his check-up, then asked Jinny to get dressed.

"Jinny, did you have natural births or caesars?"

"I had two caesars, doctor. Why do you ask?"

"Are you sure?"

"Yes, I know for a fact. When I was pregnant with my son, I told my first gynae I wanted an elective caesar. I told him the only thing I ever wanted to push in life was a pram. He told me to get another gynae, and I did!"

"Jinny, when I examined your vagina, I found a really bad, jagged tear from your vagina right through to your anus. It looks like you've had a really bad episiotomy.

"Doctor, I have never had a natural childbirth. I am aware that I have a really bad tear. It's from… The thing is, I was repeatedly attacked when I was a child. That is how I got the tear…"

He looked at her and was quiet for a while.

"Would you allow me to repair this tear for you, Jinny?"

She stared back for a while, gobsmacked.

"Yes. I would like the tear to be repaired. There has always been an element of having sex that has been painful. But I don't think my medical aid will cover labiaplasty."

"I'm not going to charge you for this. I would like to fix it for you."

"Okay. But don't I need to be under anaesthetic to have a vaginal repair?"

"That brings me to my next point Jinny. Your uterus has become a mass of tissue that is putting pressure on your sciatic nerve. That's why you have pain down your right leg. I'd like to book you into surgery tomorrow so we can give you a sub-total hysterectomy. Your uterus is not in good shape. The faster it comes out the better."

"Ohh… That's a bit radical. Can't you give me a pill or something?"

"I wish I could. But your uterus needs to come out. And sooner rather than later. Tomorrow would be a good day for it."

"Ohh… Okay...

"I'll do all the necessary booking into hospital then. And I'll see you tomorrow in theatre."

Jinny wasn't worried about losing her uterus. She didn't want any more kids anyway. But she'd heard that hysterectomies were incredibly painful. It was the pain she feared more than anything.

Sherbert, she thought. I could really do without this now. But if it has to be done, it has to be done.

She called Ryder up to tell him what was going on. Early the next morning, she drove herself to the hospital. She got there early and hopped into her allocated bed. She had just settled herself in when Ryder arrived.

"Hello, my girl!"

"Ryder, what're you doing here?"

"Well, I've come to tell the doctors not to kill you. It will be a bit difficult if two little kids pitch up on my doorstep looking like waifs and strays with suitcases and say, "Hi, Dad, Mom's died. We've come to live with you"

They both roared with laughter.

"Yes, I suppose that could be a bit problematic… But if I died, would you look after the kids for me?

"Of course I'd look after your kids. It would be a bit difficult to explain to my wife, but I would look after the kids. For sure."

Wow, she thought. He really was a decent, solid, good guy, For the first time she felt lucky to have such a wonderful person in her life.

Ryder walked with her through to the theatre doors. She heard him telling the doctors to look after her, and then he was gone.

"How do you feel Jinny?" the doctor asked.

"I don't feel ready."

"That's what most people say. But it's okay. Please just hop across from your bed onto the surgery table. Let's make you comfortable."

She lay down flat on the green sheets of the surgery table. The surgery nurses wore navy-blue outfits and white surgical masks with blue surgical shower caps. One of the nurses put a warm blanket across her body, then the anaesthetist asked her to stretch out her arm. Another nurse stepped forward and put a mask over her face. Her doctor stood by her and held her hand.

"Everything is going to be okay, Jinny. Now count to ten."

She started to count and could feel the gas relaxing her. There was a prick as the anaesthetic needle pierced her arm and the world started to fade. The last thing she said was, "Please get me safely to the other side. I've got to look after my kids…"

Then she was out.

***

JINNY WOKE UP shivering and shaking. She felt like her body was plunging down a hole. There was a nurse by her bed.

"I'm crashing," she cried. "I need to go to ICU!"

"What do you mean by crashing?"

Her entire body was numb. She couldn't move her hands or legs. She tried to sit up, but nothing would move. She could just about speak…

"Nurse, my vitals are crashing. I've had operations before and I've had the same feeling. I am crashing! You need to get me to ICU now. I've got about 30 minutes to live! If you don't get me to ICU now…"

Then she was out. She came around with two nurses at her head and another at her feet. They were pushing her bed along a corridor.

"Are you taking me to ICU?"

"Yes, sweetheart, we are. You're going to be okay. Just hang in there…"

Then she faded into sleep again.

***

JINNY CAME AROUND in ICU. The nurses were trying to transfer her from one bed to another. Her body was in absolute agony and she was shivering. It must be post-op shock. But it was okay. She was in ICU. The ICU team would fix her.

A nurse came up to the bed.

"Jinny? I'm Lina. Are you in any pain?"

"Yes."

"Don't worry, sweetheart. We're going to give you something for that."

She felt a burning sensation running up her arm. Then she faded back into blissful oblivion.

She spent what felt like ages slipping in and out of sleep. Every time she woke, the nurses asked if she was in pain. She said yes, and they would give her another shot of something to take the pain away. By late afternoon, she was able to sit up. Thanks to the pain shots, she was flying around like a kite.

Ryder came to visit her with a pot of flowers. He was so considerate – he knew she hated bouquets. It reminded her of when her husband had died. Everyone had brought her bunches of flowers and they had all died, just like him.

"Hello, my girl. How are you feeling?"

"I am so happy, Ryder," she smiled.

"I can see that, my girl. Why are you so happy?"

"I got a new fanny!"

Ryder looked at her for a few seconds, aghast. He asked the nurse if she'd given her a lot of painkillers today.

"Sweetheart, I think you must be mistaken. You had a hysterectomy today."

She grinned at him through her drug haze.

"I know, Ryder. But I also got a new fanny. He said… I wanted to tell you… My fanny was torn when I was raped as a child. The doctor did a hysterectomy and he also fixed my fanny."

"Good heavens, Jinny!"

"I'm so happy. I am not broken any more. I have a fixed fanny!"

Ryder patted her on the hand.

"Okay, my girl. I'm glad you're all fixed up now…" The she drifted off again.

****

JINNY SPENT FOUR days in ICU before being released. The doctor told her to take it easy for at least six weeks.

She just felt really, really tired. But apart from that, she felt well, and happy. There was something about having her fanny fixed that made her happy. It felt like the disgrace and shame of being violated as a child had been taken away.

There really were good men in the world – and her gynae was one of them. He had fixed one of the injustices she had been dished out. She didn't feel broken on the inside any more.

She felt flushed with a new determination. She was going to book a few more sessions with Jonathan. And she was going to get the life she had always wanted for her and her kids. To hell with Stockholm Syndrome! She wanted her own home and her kids and a normal life.

****

SHE SCHEDULED HER next session with Jonathan. But she found that she didn't want to talk about how she felt. Truth be told, she felt messed up. She preferred to talk about what she needed to do to get her life sorted out. Jonathan recommended the following:

First of all, she needed to get some GPS co-ordinates of her own. Sleeping on a friend's couch wasn't good for her. Even if it was a tiny one-bedroomed cottage, she needed to find somewhere with good energy, where she felt safe. That sounded right. She missed having her own little space. Jinny wasn't too sure how she was going to pull it off, but she could start looking around.

Then, she needed to get another opinion on her divorce. It sounded like her estranged husband didn't really want to divorce her. He just wanted to financially cripple her. Making her suffer made him feel vindicated. This made complete sense, the only trouble was that once you were in the legal system it was difficult to get out. Especially when you were the one who had filed for the divorce. If you retracted the divorce, you were then liable for all legal costs. Also, there was no way that Jinny wanted to stay married to Justin.

Thirdly, she needed to make a choice and stick to one guy. Jumping between different guys was not good for her either. Yes this made sense – she couldn't stand the guilt and shame of being a "serial monogamist".

Finally, she needed to consider taking a break from counselling for a while. That way she could sort out her personal issues and concentrate on the Safe Spaces project. That should earn her income and would make a difference to a lot of people's lives. She wouldn't have to directly counsel people until she could stabilise her life. That felt good to Jinny too. She was tired of trying to be a successful person on the outside and feeling like a wreck on the inside.

When Jinny walked out of her consultation with Jonathan she realised how silly she had been, trying to deal with all of her issues herself. If she had just sought help sooner, she might not have got herself into such a pickle in the first place.

She was going to start trawling Gumtree for a little place for herself. Then, when she was settled, she was going to bring her babies home. Skyla had told her ages ago, "Mommy, I don't care where we live. I just want to be with you. I would even live in the desert in a tent with you if we could be together."

She called Aiden and asked for another meeting. She told him she had some personal issues she needed help with.

Aiden said, "Sure, let's meet tomorrow."

Tomorrow seemed a bit soon, but Jinny knew that once she got the ball of change rolling in her life everything was going to happen quickly.

She met Aiden at his offices.

"So what can I help you with?"

"Well, there are few things about my life that I haven't shared with you. I'd like to share them with you now, in the hope that you will be able to assist me."

"Go right ahead. I'm all ears."

"We had a rather unusual start to our friendship. First of all, with you being my client, then firing me, then us having sundowners at your house… And then we kissed and I left in a rush. Then that Safe Spaces meeting…"

"Yes, if you put it that way, we did get off to a bit of an unusual start. And while we're on the subject, why did you stop at a kiss that night?"

She squirmed in her seat, but she owed Aiden an answer.

"Well, there are few reasons, Aiden. You're a good man and you deserve to be with a good girl. I'm not financially stable, and I don't think it was fair of me to get involved with you knowing I'm on the skids at the moment. And the last reason is because although I have been single and filed for a divorce four years ago, I'm still legally married."

"Oh…"

"Yes… To a man who behaves like a psychopath. And I know how much you value honesty and loyalty. Unfortunately, in the space I've been in, I have had neither of these qualities.

Aiden had his stern face on.

"Jinny, I always had the feeling that we have been put into each other's lives to help one another. Not necessarily to date one another. So it's okay. I am 41 and I've never been married. That's kind of worse than being 42 and trying to get divorced!"

"How can that be worse, Aiden?"

"Well, when you're 41 and you've never been married, people start to wonder if there's something seriously wrong with you," he laughed.

"Well, I'm 42 and I've been married twice. My first husband killed himself and I seriously wish my second husband would do the same thing! But it doesn't seem like the second husband is going to die any time soon. I don't think even God wants him!"

And they both laughed this time.

"I don't believe in God, Jinny."

"Well, I do."

"How has God helped you, Jinny?"

"For one thing, I think he sent us to each other to help each other."

"Well, I don't believe that exactly, but I do want to help you."

"Okay, I am not going to argue with you. But I would pray for you if you were ill or died, Aiden"

"I wouldn't pray for you. I'm not the praying type"

"Okay."

"What do you need help with, Jinny?"

She took a deep breath and told Aiden what had happened to her and her kids in trying to get divorced. How she had lost everything financially, how the estranged ex and his girlfriend had impacted on her ability to earn, how the kids were living with her parents, and how she was sleeping on a couch at Carol's place. She told him how she was no closer to finalising the divorce now than she had been four years ago, but she was financially more broken than she had been before she had filed for a divorce. And that the divorce wasn't going to be finalised any time soon because her ex would not agree to it. She didn't have the money to fight for the divorce and she didn't even have a maintenance order in place to help her look after the kids.

"All right, Jinny. There is quite a lot I can do to help you, but you're not going to like what I have to say."

"Out with it."

"You're being stupid. The height of stupidity is doing the same thing and expecting a different result. It's clear that your ex really doesn't want the divorce because he doesn't want to let go of control of you. So stop trying to divorce him! Who cares if you're still married! He's been living with his girlfriend and their baby for the last four years. You've had no contact with him and you have no intention of going back to him. Any man who falls in love with you will be able to see this for himself!

"Secondly, let's get you the maintenance that you need to support the kids. You can apply for this yourself at the Magistrate's Court. You don't need legal representation to get that sorted, but I will help you get the paper work in place. Then you can go through and apply for the maintenance yourself. You've already represented yourself twice in the High Court and won, so you'll be able to handle yourself in the Magistrate's Court. I will send one of my candidate attorneys to sit with you so you don't have to be on your own."

Wow, she thought, wow, wow, wow!

"Thanks Aiden! Wow! We also need to discuss how I'm going to pay you. I am on the bones of my butt at the moment…"

"Jinny, please don't stress about that now. Let's get your maintenance sorted out and then we can come to a monthly arrangement for you to pay me."

"Thank you, Aiden. Thank you!"

"It's a pleasure, Jinny. You should have told me ages ago what was going on."

"I know I should have. But I've always found it hard to talk about my personal stuff. I'd much rather help people with their issues than deal with my own. It's kind of like 'the shoemaker's children never have shoes' scenario."

"It's okay, Jinny I'm going to help you get yourself back on track. You're a good person."

"Thanks again, Aiden."

As Jinny stood to shake his hand she felt completely bowled over that he would go out of his way to help her!

***

SHE HAD HEARD over and over again over the last four years that the court is not a court of emotion. It is a court of law. It felt like the court was not a place of God either. How was it possible that the judges had allowed her legal matters to run on for so long and not put a stop to it? There should be a moratorium on how long you were allowed to drag out a divorce. She felt disappointed that she was not going to be able to get legally divorced, but at the end of the day, the wellbeing of her kids was more important.

Okay, so she was still looking for a place to stay. She'd had the first meeting to get the legal side of things sorted out. Now she needed to address her personal life.

On the relationship front, it wasn't really rocket science. She must never call Christiaan again. She didn't love him; he didn't love her. It had been nothing more than sex that felt good at the time. But strangely Jinny had always felt ashamed, guilty and dirty afterwards. God knows why, because they had always used condoms and sex with condoms didn't feel like real sex anyway. The only relationship she really needed to think through was the one with Ryder.

Ryder had gone from being someone who had saved her from being injured at her charity event years ago, to someone who had saved her life. In the last few years he had stood by her, talked issues through with her and become a good mentor. Jinny was certain she would have taken that steak knife out of the kitchen drawer and run into a wall ages ago if it hadn't been for Ryder talking her through things in his own way.

On the sex side of things, he had gone from being someone she was going to teach a lesson, to someone who'd taught her many new life lessons. Their sex life had started out as angry, wild sexcapades in hotel rooms, then moved onto decadent treats at health hydros and bridal suites, to sex at home on couches and beds and in showers… And strangely enough, after her hysterectomy, Ryder had overnight become an incredibly gentle and attentive lover. Which had thrilled Jinny! He had massaged her back and fondled her and spent ages on fingering her – and then had been upset when she didn't come. She'd made the excuse that she was tired and maybe it was too soon after the hysterectomy. She hadn't told him that him talking about his wife the entire way through their foreplay had put her off her stride and made her feel second rate.

Cunnilingus was never going to be Ryder's thing, although they had both got the giggles a while back when Jinny had told him that she really missed oral sex. He had pitched up with a tub of caramel yoghurt. He said he planned slapping it onto her vadge and then would try to lick it off. She'd burst out laughing and had told him there was no ways he was putting food on her vadge. But she appreciated the thought and the effort he had made to please her. She hadn't bothered to mention that she felt a bit mortified and hurt, because obviously he didn't like the sight or the taste or smell of her vagina. She would never ask for tongue again.

On the friendship side of things, Ryder was the only person who'd ever taken the time to get to know her. Ryder had loved her first because she'd given him hell in the beginning. Any man in his right mind would have walked away and never looked back.

Ryder and Jinny had been through a lot together, but at no time had they shouted at each other. Usually if they gave each other a bit of space they were able to address their issues. Neither of them was mean or malicious and neither of them wanted to cause harm to each other's families. In fact, they would both go out of their way to protect their families.

In truth, she had never been loved by a man until she met Ryder. Not even her first husband had gone out of his way to understand her and stand by her like Ryder had. And the hardest part was that Ryder was not in a position to claim her as his own.

He had sent an email a while ago that left no doubt that Ryder loved her but that he was bound by duty and tradition. Jinny would never ask him to leave his wife, but she would like to be a steady lover in his life. She wanted to spend the rest of her children's childhood focussing on them and her work, and have Ryder as a steady friend and lover without the everyday demands of a husband. But that was not what Ryder wanted for her. That was clear from his email. He had mentioned a few times over the years that Jinny loved him more than he loved her – and Jinny had felt that knife twisting in her heart again."

From: Ryder Parker<RParkerJ@safrec.org.za>
To: Me

___

Dear Jinny
 "You left me quite moved and humbled yesterday and you've been very much on my mind ever since.
Thank you for the beautiful note – you really do have a beautiful way with words and manage to express yourself with kindness and love. An extraordinary thing, given your history to date.

I was distressed with myself as I realised I had inadvertently got you into a position I had been trying not to – our feelings for each other are not supposed to get in the way of your longer-term happiness and security. Ever.

I will (I hope) always be there for you and be your very special and close friend and hope to be a pillar of strength and security for you as you finally separate from your awful past.
But I'm not going to run away as you find a new love in your life and someone to be 'the Dad' for your chickens, as they need that stability and father figure in their lives at this important time. I can't be that selfish and with my wife and my chickens I could never fill that role, although I do think I could be a favourite uncle maybe...?

Don't let good opportunities slip you by.

Yours always,

Ryder

___

She knew that if a man said he did not love you that much, you should believe him. The worst thing anyone could do was live in the hope of getting someone to love you more. The reality was, that never happened!

She was a stupid, stupid, stupid girl for still wanting to have Ryder in her life.

Maybe this was what Ryder had meant when he had told her years ago that, "You are better than this, Jinny."

"You deserve better."

"You are worth more than what you are getting."

When he had said he would like to walk her down the aisle at her next wedding… but wanted to know if he could have one last shag before she got married, they had both laughed again. Then Ryder's tone had changed and he'd looked sad.

"Because in the end I am going to be the one who will get hurt more than you, Jinny. Because you're going to get on with your life and you're going to have a wonderful life and I will be the one left behind as you move on with your life. I will never tell you to go away, Jinny."

Why couldn't Ryder come to terms with the fact it was possible to have both? Why did he always feel he needed to choose between duty and happiness? Why did he feel that having Jinny as a steady girlfriend on the side would mean he would have to forsake his wife on the other? Frenchmen had wives and lovers. Why couldn't he?

Jinny knew that Ryder was exceptionally traditional and typically English duty bound. He was the only man she had a good history with; who she had a memory bank full of happy experiences with; who had taken the time to get to know her and tried to understand her; who would have looked after her kids if she had died; and who had wanted her to be more than what she had become. He had stood by her. Jinny knew it was selfish of Ryder to be involved with her when he was married – but he was also unselfish enough to want her to have more than a boyfriend on the side.

***

IF JINNY HAD to look at the hardcore reality of it, Ryder didn't really want her.

In South African society there was an unspoken and unwritten culture that put pressure on her to "settle down and find a man". But she was not ready to find a man and she was not ready to let go of Ryder. She had never felt like asking him to go away either. But he had never been hers and he had never wanted her to be his.

Ryder had his own level of dysfunction and disappointments with the way his life had turned out. But he was a good man at heart and he had shown Jinny in his own way that there were good men in the world. He had taught her that it was okay to speak up about things you did not like in a relationship, that issues could be handled without being screamed at, belittled, humiliated or beaten. That having a friendship with your man is just as important as having a big dick and behaving like one too. Jinny knew now that she deserved to be handled with kindness, consideration and respect. Somehow, in between the mess of everything Jinny had experienced, she'd learned what it was to be loved and respected.

Once, after Justin had beaten her, Jinny had prayed for the Lord to just send her one good man to love her – and he had. She should have prayed, "Lord please send me one good, single man to love me. Forever."

She was not entirely at peace with God in general. It said in the Bible, "Suffer the little children to come unto me" But Jinny had really suffered in her childhood, and if God was so powerful, why had he allowed her and countless other children to suffer? Jinny didn't understand God and why he had allowed her to be attacked when she was little. But she felt that God had sent her Ryder, which was exactly what she had needed. And maybe in a way Ryder had needed a project and a young energy too. Maybe he was processing his own fear and his own reality that his wife would pass on.

Jinny knew that the punishment for having extramarital relationships was not only the fear of getting caught out but always worrying if you were the only "extra" in your partner's life - always having to sneak around and never being able to introduce your love as your partner in public.

It would take a while for her to recover from the Stockholm Syndrome. Jinny didn't know if she would ever truly recover, but for now she wanted to focus on her finances and her kids and things that made her feel happy and safe. And she wanted to enjoy the time she had with Ryder.

She knew things would have to change with her and Ryder and that if she ever found another man to love she wanted to be loved in her entirety, for all that she is and everything that she wanted to be, by one good man.

You can't choose the life you're dished out, but you can choose to survive and to make the best of it.

***

JINNY: A PSYCHOLOGICAL PROFILE

Leonard Carr, psychologist

JINNY'S STORY HIGHLIGHTS in a very graphic way how the sexual abuse and exploitation of a child deforms the child's developing personality and robs her of her innocent view of the world.

An innocent view of the world is one where you take people at their word, accept and offer love with open-hearted grace, and trust they have your interests at heart and will not deliberately cause you harm. Not having to second guess your own experience and self-expression or the motives and intentions of others allows you to be natural, open and spontaneous in your relationships.

Once betrayed and robbed of that innocence, the child has to forever be alert for signs of hidden agendas, power plays and malintent. She needs to treat all interactions as manipulating and controlling others, either implicitly or explicitly, in order to feel safe and in control.

The currency of abuse is sex and power. A child sexualised for the purpose of providing the adult with a sense of power and gratification learns to see relationships as transactional and arranged around control and exploitation.

Deep inside this little girl, who is forced into pseudo maturity and premature adulthood to survive, is a vulnerable scared child who craves protection, nurturing and unconditional love. She becomes caught between two violently opposing psychological needs. The one is to dominate, control and take revenge on men in a sexually sadistic manner. The other is the longing to surrender into the arms of a strong, loving mate who will cherish and look after her unconditionally.

Her feelings after acting out her angry, untrusting side through the domination and humiliation of Ryder were followed by feelings of self-loathing and disgust and sadness at having hurt her potential source of love. When she acts out her need to surrender and be taken care of, her fear kicks in and makes her want to pull away or sabotage the relationship – or reposition it into her exercise of sexual domination.

If you have learned through the messages you received while being violated and exploited by a man, that no matter what a man tells you about love or caring about you, all he wants to do is get into your pants, then sex is the only communication that you truly trust.

Caught in the teeth of this double bind, Jinny is lost to the world of intimacy, and of sexuality being about bonding, mutual pleasuring and deepening of emotional connection. So far is Jinny from this world, that she cannot even stay connected and intimate. She is removed from the experience where her own feelings of tenderness, vulnerability and the ambiguity and uncertainty of a relationship unfold in a natural way that leads organically to sex.

At the slightest discomfort, she starts to use sexual play and banter to test out her man with suggestions and to lure him onto her own territory where she can control the outcome – as opposed to allowing him to initiate and invite her onto his turf where she implicitly believes he will ambush and overpower her.

It makes perfect sense for Jinny to project her inner child onto the world and go in search of her safe place by creating and living in it vicariously through the people she helps.

It is clear from the story that Jinny's healing journey is only just beginning.

***

Sins of Abuse
by Leonard Carr

"ABUSE USUALLY HAPPENS in the context of family relationships, or at least between people known to each other. When the perpetrator is a family member or an authority figure, like a teacher or a religious leader, it is often a challenge to get people to acknowledge that the line has been crossed and that the nature of the interactions constitutes abuse.

When abuse happens within families or communities, there are often vested interests that would be better served by denying or ignoring abuse in order to protect those in power. This results in authority figures ignoring or minimising the seriousness of the allegation, appeasing the victim or even outright shaming and threatening the victim into silence.

It is the fear of being disqualified, made to feel invisible, punished or shamed that discourages victims from speaking up and admitting to having been abused, let alone confronting the perpetrator.

Abuse happens because the people closest to the victim or people responsible for the protection of people in their charge often choose to ignore or turn a blind eye to situations and people who potentially pose a threat. People also often fail to question changes in the behaviour and demeanour of a family member, friend, student or work associate and never ask if something may be wrong or troubling them.

Every indifferent person who could reach out to or protect a victim and does not, as well as every person who knows that someone is in distress and does nothing, shares some responsibility for the abuse happening in their midst.

Abusers and bullies in general tend to lack empathy and compassion by nature. It is the passive and silent bystanders who have those abilities and could use those sensitivities to impel them into positive action, who hold the power to prevent tragedy.

Nowhere to hide
Conservative religious communities try to insulate themselves from such threats in the vain attempt to eliminate such people and the threat they pose to their seemingly pristine worlds. The problem is that these people exist amongst them, often camouflaged in religious garb. They cynically exploit the often naïve kindness of the community who make them welcome in the name of compassion and mercy to a stranger. There are taboos against sexual misconduct, inappropriate relationships and sexual acts in most traditional societies and religions.

Shame – Stealing the humanity of another

All abuse involves a level of diminishing and degrading others and turning them into objects to be used for the fulfilment of the needs or desires of the perpetrators. This theft of someone's basic humanity is the ultimate crime against another, because it is an affront to and an attack on the image of G-d within that person. Shaming causes a sense in the victim that his/her existence has no intrinsic value. This leaves the person with feelings of overwhelming, all-consuming worthlessness, self-hatred, disgust and despair. It is a feeling of being reduced to something insignificant and even detestable. Shame is the sense of one's being, one's existence and all that one values and holds dear being negated.

It is so destructive, that in shame people often want to finish the job by disappearing, by hiding or even dying, which aligns the physical and the spiritual and emotional reality. When people shame others and do not in turn feel ashamed of their actions, it shows total disregard and indifference to the humanity of others. It is as if the one shamed is worth so little in reality that remorse for one's own actions would be redundant, an overreaction.

Theft

All dehumanising practices rob people of aspects of their being that contribute to their sense of wholeness. Examples are power, self-esteem, dignity, a sense of self-worth, a sense of innocence and purity.

Lying and creating false impressions

The dehumanising practices that constitute abuse are forms of manipulation of the other person's sense of reality in order to win their trust and compliance or to threaten them through fear of being shamed or punished, as if it is the victim's fault for being abused.

Perpetrators take advantage of the naivety or ignorance or innocence of another through creating false impressions and lying. All perpetrators coerce victims into giving up their power and autonomy by coercing them into disbelieving their own feelings, knowledge and inner experience.

Predators, through a masterfully conniving set of well-practised techniques, recruit their victims into their web of control, like a fishermen pulling on the rod, encountering resistance and letting go and then overcoming the resistance by craftily pulling again, slowing reeling in the fish.

This grooming would happen by them making an inappropriate suggestion or pushing some other boundary and then apologising for offending the victim who, being polite or a compliant people-pleaser, replies politely that it is okay. Through the mixing of messages, pushing boundaries and then feigning care and remorse the predator gets the victim to drop her guard because she becomes too confused to discern positive from threatening interactions.

In time the victim stops trusting in her own reactions and instincts, because what feels bad or wrong is cleverly reframed by the predator as good. By the time the bad is unambiguous, the victim becomes too afraid or ashamed to tell her loved ones or friends. This is also because at this stage the predator, now fully in control, is openly and brazenly threatening.

Destruction of Potential
When people are abused, they change often fundamentally and permanently through the loss of the innocence that existed before they were violated. This change affects the way they see themselves, the world, their relationships and their own destiny or potential in life. When you rob someone of any aspect of their being then you are destroying the potential that could have arisen from that aspect of themselves.

While it is true that people can grow from adversity and that hardship can bring out even more potential in a person, this does not excuse perpetrators from culpability for their actions.

An example of how a lifetime of potential can be destroyed can be seen in people who have been sexually abused. They may choose not to marry, and if they do, they may avoid or not enjoy physical intimacy. This causes the marital bond to be compromised, which in turn undermines the closeness and unity needed to build true peace and unity in their homes. This can and often does lead to divorce or a life time of dissatisfaction.

A person's identity, lifestyle and sense of self may become shaped around trying to deal with the abusive experience. This can result in avoiding pain through addiction, isolation or attempts to regain what was taken away in the abuse by engaging in alternative sexual lifestyles or re-enacting the original experience sometimes through abusing others.

Healing – Victims are never to blame
Persons who have been violated, dehumanised or shamed need to be reassured unequivocally they are not to blame for what happened to them, even if they were in some way coerced to co-operate with the perpetrator and thus feel like they were complicit.

The framework that can be used to illustrate how to help people to heal from abuse can be built by restoring to the victim whatever was taken away from him/her through the abuse.

The responsibility for helping with healing falls on all of those who have the ability or agency to restore the power, the dignity and the sense of self-worth to victims."

Excerpt taken from the article Sins of Abuse by Leonard Carr.

RELATIONSHIP SURVIVAL GUIDE

Should you wish to learn more about toxic relationships, how to survive them and the practical and legal aspects of moving on, visit Ali's website at www.alimurray.com. The short book **Relationship Survival Guide – Surviving Heartache And Toxic Relationships** is available as a free download at www.alimurray.co.za/relationship-survival-guide.php.

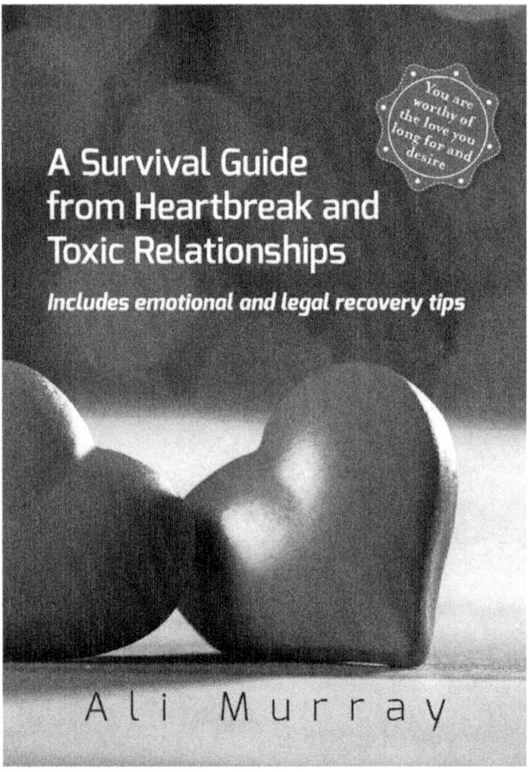

Go online to subscribe to our free newsletter: www.alimurray.com

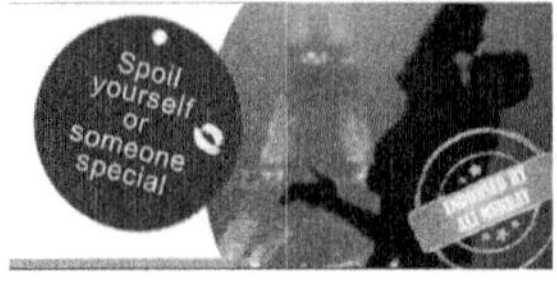

Order a signed copy of the book:
www.alimurray.com

Printed in Great Britain
by Amazon